Social Pollination

*Escape the Hype of Social Media
and Join the Companies Winning At It*

Monica L. O'Brien

Library of Congress Cataloging-in-Publication Data is avaliable.

ISBN 978-0-9842348-0-6

Spaulding House Publishing
2616 N. Spaulding Avenue
Chicago, IL 60647

Printed in the United States of America

First printing

Author: Monica O'Brien
Editor: Jay Wigley

Disclaimer: This material is provided "as is" without any warranty of any kind. Every effort has been made to enssure the accuracy of this book; however, errors and omissions may occur. The publisher assumes no responsibility for any damages arising from the use of this book.

Acknowledgments

When I first told my mom about this book, her main concern was not what I would write within the pages, but rather what I planned to write on the acknowledgments page.

So I guess I should start by saying thank you to my parents, for raising me to be independent and supporting me when I take unconventional risks that most parents would frown at.

Thank you to Seth Godin, Tim Ferriss, and Gini Dietrich for contributing excerpts to this book.

Thank you to my editor Jay Wigley for reminding me that every project in the world has a totally ridiculous timeline.

Thank you to all my friends, online and offline, who have read, shared, and supported my blog for the past two years. You've challenged me to work and think harder than I ever have in my life. This book would not be possible without you.

And above all, thank you to my husband, Eric, who believes in me and tolerates all the evenings I spend reading and writing.

Contents

Goals and Strategy   25

Choose Your Social Media Channels   43

Build Your Platform   73

The Psychology of Online Sharing 97

Content Ideas 113

Optimize Your Content 125

PR and Advertising 143

Introduction

Today's internet is interactive and information is free-flowing like never before. With hundreds of interactive sites, anyone can post comments, pictures, videos, and articles--all for free. In addition to the large networking sites like Facebook, Twitter, and LinkedIn, there are also smaller networking sites that are focused on niche interests.

Years ago, you needed an online store to make money on the internet. Today, you only need a brand--a strong, authentic brand that people can trust.

But this is not a book about how trusting relationships have become important to business.

I am not going to waste your time by explaining how relationships, authenticity, and trust are important in business. What I want to teach, however, is how to use social media tools to **scale** the idea of relationships and trust.

Simple math shows that as an individual or small company, you cannot establish a one-to-one relationship with every customer. But that does not mean that those individuals you cannot reach personally should not be your customers. Rather, those people, to become your customers, will need to hear about you in the context of a relationship based on trust. In other words, your company must build trust with consumers using referrals and recommendations.

Referrals and recommendations can come in many forms-- a link, a comment, or a casual online conversation. Social media makes it easy to find and spread referrals and recommendations, which is why it's a powerful tool for growing any business.

With social media, you don't need to market your products constantly; instead, you need to cultivate brand enthusiasts who will market your products for you. This book teaches you how to find and nurture communities of people who love your brand and would love to help you build brand awareness, for little to no cost on your part.

Entrepreneurs know ideas are worth NOTHING without implementation. Relax! Anyone who understands the basics of how to use technology can implement my system.

What is social pollination?

Social pollination is simply brands and organizations populating social media sites with content to let the message spread further than traditional marketing techniques would allow. In the past, company websites were a place for people to learn about brands; now, people turn to social media sites for this information. In response, companies are creating content that can be shared easily across social platforms.

Former Forrester Research analyst and web strategist Jeremiah Owyang explains, "Trusted conversations have fragmented to the social web - shifting the balance of power to communities." Social pollination is about embracing the power of communities and using it to your advantage.

Why I wrote this book

After several consulting gigs with startups, I noticed a trend in the types of mistakes small companies made with social media.

I also noticed that most social media books and case studies were geared towards large companies and big picture ideas. I wanted to create a book for small companies (or entrepreneurial teams within large companies) who wanted concrete, step-by-step instructions for creating and executing a social media strategy.

Here are 15 mistakes small companies make with social media - are you making them too?

Not developing a social media strategy

Because social media is the hottest trend in marketing, companies assume that all they have to do is set up a Twitter account and a Facebook fan page. This is the equivalent of pulling random magazines out of off the rack and purchasing full page color ad in each one, then throwing together a quick and dirty PowerPoint flyer to run. Just like any other communication medium, social media requires a well-thought out marketing strategy plan.

Perfecting a social media strategy

Even though a social media strategy is important, don't wait for the strategy to set up your company's accounts.

Reserving your company's name on various social media sites is of the utmost importance. Furthermore, because it takes time to build social media accounts, every minute you waste by not showing up is followers you could be losing.

Thinking the tools are everything

Most social media talk revolves around tools – ie: 10 Ways to Get More Followers on Twitter. While it's useful to get into the details and tactics of social media, a solid marketing strategy should work no matter the medium. The smartest companies will focus on strategy because in the world of Web 2.0, the tools are constantly changing.

Not using the tools correctly

It takes a long time to build credibility, especially as a company because individuals are taught to be wary of anything that looks like marketing or spamming. Unfortunately, it only takes one discrepancy to do damage to a company's reputation. Err on the side of caution with each tool, and take time to listen to the conversations and learn the etiquette for each medium.

Not using the tools at all

Many corporate social media profiles make the company look like it went out of business, because the company doesn't update regularly. Every tool holds opportunity for companies, so companies must be willing to experiment. Rest assured your competitors will be experimenting, so don't let them set the tone or build equity online without having your own presence.

Putting all eggs in one basket

It's exciting to see extraordinary results on one form of social media, and tempting to invest all your resources into what's working. Try to resist. With the speed at which technology changes, social media is starting to look similar to the fashion cycle: one day you're in, the next day you're out. Tools fall in and out of fashion all the time – remember Friendster? (I didn't think so.) Companies that build a large equity on one tool will find themselves with nothing if the tool loses popularity.

Gathering followers rather than building a network

There are no shortcuts in social media, and the bottom line is companies have to build relationships with their customers before they can sell anything. Social media may seem free, but there are hidden time costs to build relationships. Social media is not a quick way to make more sales; in fact, social media actually adds cycle time to the sales process. Just like any other process, a company must consider how much of its resources to invest.

Putting the horse before the carriage

Another cliché is the company that doesn't follow a logical process with social media and then wonders why it isn't seeing results. Common sense comes in handy here. For example, consider a company that doesn't currently have many customers, but creates a Facebook fan page and starts promoting it with Facebook ads. The keyword is "fan;" people who haven't experienced the product are not likely to join a fan club for it. Make sure your company is following a logical customer acquisition process by thinking about social media from the user-perspective.

Pitching poorly

Every social media user has a very clear idea of what social media means to them, and how they want to be approached by companies on social media. Most companies don't realize that the **way** they approach social media sends its own message to consumers.

Creating impersonal accounts

Users don't follow companies; they follow engaging people who work at companies. Unless the tool is meant specifically for companies to use (ie: Facebook fan pages), every account should be an actual person who has a name and a title that clearly signifies him or her as a face of the company. This person should write with a conversational tone and respond to other participants in the conversation. Automated accounts or accounts that are updated with a stream of links do not produce results.

Controlling the message

Social media is not about controlling a message. In fact, the very nature of social media is such that no one person or organization can control the message. Because social media is a medium to share information through a network, companies must realize that once they put the message out there, they have no control anymore. Users can choose to edit the message, inject their own opinions into the message, share the message, or ignore the message. Furthermore, companies can't even control where the message starts: a user can also create a message about a company without having any affiliation to them. Because of the nature of social media, companies that try to control the message will have difficulty reaping any of the benefits of the medium.

Not controlling the message

While companies should be careful about trying to exercise too much control over the message, there is also the opposite end of the spectrum to avoid. Companies often cite "control over message" as a reason not to participate in social media, but the truth is that companies have lost control of the message whether they participate or not. This is because, as mentioned earlier, users can create a message and drive the conversation surrounding that message.

So how can companies exercise some control over a message and still reap the benefits of social media (rapid diffusion of information through people sharing messages with their networks)? The answer is that companies need to participate in the conversation. Responding to complaints and stressing the benefits and what the company does well; these are all ways for companies to control the end-consumer's perception of its products.

Abusing permission

Abusing permission is by far one of the worst mistakes a company can make with messaging. An example would be if a company collected emails from various blogs in a certain niche and started sending weekly newsletters. While this seems harmless on the surface, none of these bloggers signed up for the company's weekly emails, and thus have not requested the information.

Abusing permission is a fast way for companies to lose credibility, damage relationships, and generally make a bad name for themselves in social media. So where do you draw the line with abusing permission?

Unfortunately, this question is similar to asking where comedians draw the line with potentially offensive jokes. The truth is that different users have different levels of tolerance. Just like a comedian might experiment with messaging based on the feedback he or she is receiving from the audience, your company must experiment with the right level of communication, erring on the side of unobtrusive.

Not measuring results

Social media campaign measurement is one of the most important things a business can do. If you are doing sales calls, you know exactly how many people you call per day and what the conversion rate is. Why should social media be any different?

Social media is simply another form of communication, just like calling someone on the phone or meeting someone in person. Companies measure communication on social media the same way it is measured in other formats.

Misinterpreting the concept of scale

Many companies wonder about the scale of social media. People say, "Building relationships one person at a time - that seems like a lot of work for just one sale!"

The truth is that social media is simply a communication tool that gives people a way to talk about products and services. Essentially, social media is about word-of-mouth, except you can reach a larger group of people because on social media, information flows between close friends as easily as it flows between mere aquaintances.

Word-of-mouth is probably one of the most scalable forms of

marketing on the planet. With advertising you are only guaranteed to reach a certain audience once because there is no sharing involved. When you create a message that is shared over and over again, it spreads quickly like a virus and gives you more reach than you could get with traditional advertising methods.

This means social media is highly scalable as well. It takes time to develop word-of-mouth, which is why you may not see results on social media right away; but trust me, this stuff is powerful once you get the ball rolling!

If you follow the guidelines within this book, you can avoid making these mistakes and learn what to do instead!

What you will learn in this book

- The 7 business goals social media is best suited for

- How to create a social media strategy that makes sense for your business goals

- Which specific platforms YOU should build a presence on

- The 12 social media success factors and how you can optimize them to go viral using any social media tool

- How to create content that people want to share

- How publicity and advertising can improve your results

- Advanced techniques to measure your social media campaigns

- How to build a social media team and optimize your time with social media

Let's get started!

You Need Others to Share Your Message

When teen princess Selena Gomez and her band The Scene launched their first album, Kiss and Tell, they knew they had to find a way to help people get the word out. At 17 years old, Selena Gomez was a Barney and Friends veteran and starred on a successful TV show on the Disney Channel. Although she received plenty of airtime through shows, movies, and celebrity news outlets, Gomez was not particularly known for her singing skills, which would prove to be an obstacle in promoting her album.

Even with repeated exposure of the first single, "Falling Down," on Radio Disney and the Disney Channel, the band still needed to utilize social pollination to create a cost-effective campaign. Luckily, Gomez had an online platform in place to spread the word. Her Facebook page had over 3 million fans, and because she had been on Twitter (and updating regularly) for several months, she had accumulated over 1 million followers by the album release.

Just having a platform is not enough; Gomez and the band also launched two major initiatives to get people buzzing about the album online. First, they held a contest through Gomez's Facebook page, urging users to upload photos or video of how they were helping to promote Kiss and Tell. "Need an idea?" the campaign asks. "Make a poster and hang it up around your school or create a t-shirt promoting Selena's album." Gomez then handpicked 10 finalists, and let the fans vote on the winners.

The second initiative was to offer a limited online preview of the album to fans who attended a listening party. Fans could listen to the full album on repeat at the Kiss and Tell website, but they had to gain admission first. To access the album, fans needed to post a message to Facebook or Twitter encouraging their friends to listen also.

Three days after the album was released, Selena Gomez tweeted about a 5-hour CD signing, where she autographed nearly five thousand CDs in one sitting. There's no doubt both these campaigns contributed to the success of the album, for several reasons:

- Gomez used her exposure in traditional media to build a platform on social media, using special content and engaging her fans with candid photos and music lyrics she was listening to

- Gomez focused on only two social media channels – Facebook and Twitter, where most of her fans already had accounts

- For the contest, Gomez provided incentives for her fans that money couldn't necessarily buy –personal phone calls with the band and a free trip for 4 to meet Gomez for the grand prize winner

- The contest not only gave fans a reason to talk about the album, but it was also easy and accessible, and allowed users to personalize their entries

- Because Gomez's singing skills were in question, consumers needed an easy way to experience the product before purchasing, which was accomplished through the listening party

- By having listeners post about the album to a social network, Gomez was able to generate buzz and stimulate sharing – which meant more people to experience the music

All of these ideas will be touched on multiple times throughout the book in detail. What's important to know now is that social pollination works – and it can work for your company too.

While we may not be famous, there's no question that we all want more word-of-mouth marketing and referrals from our network. That's why social media sounds like a dream – we put the message out there and other people get the message out.

Well, it's not quite that easy. It's harder than ever to get the attention of consumers, so only those companies that have great products and are dedicated to social media will reap the benefits.

But first, let's make a few things clear. Social media is **not** the best way to promote your business in **all** circumstances. You will probably not suddenly get millions of eyes on your product by just setting up a Twitter account, and it's not likely you will create a YouTube video that rivals the popularity of Miss Teen California's. Social media seems easy, but it is hard, hard work. Don't launch a social media campaign unless you are dedicated to its success.

When you look at potential mediums for sharing a message, social media still ranks rather low compared to mainstream media. TV shows, movies, and radio are still the best ways to get brand awareness, as many books become heavy best-sellers after becoming movies, and product placement on TV shows is at an all-time high.

That said: if you are a struggling entrepreneur, small business owner, or consultant/freelancer, you can use social media to double or triple your customer base.

How? Because it's all relative. If you are a huge company, you have the advertising budget to reach many more people through traditional advertisements than you can through social media. But if you are a little guy, social media is a good place to be. You can accomplish a lot with just time and effort, rather than with a large budget.

Why companies must use social media

If social media is not the best way for large companies to reach consumers, why are large companies still getting into the social media game? The answer is that digital content and social media are the future of marketing communications. I know you may have heard that before, but consider how:

- 25% of search engine results on the World's Top 20 largest brands are linked to user-generated content like blog posts and YouTube videos

- 35% of book sales on Amazon are the digital eBook version for the Kindle

- Social media marketing spend is expected to double between now and 2014, according to Forrester Research

In contrast, traditional advertising is dying.

- 90% of people that can Tivo (skip) through ads do so

- Only 18% of TV campaigns generate positive ROI

- Traditional advertising expenditures continue to decline, while digital advertising grows

Why is social media so important? Why do we need individual people to spread our message one-to-one now more than ever? The answer is complicated, but in short, there is a fundamental shift in the way the world is communicating. Consumers are demanding **more** from the companies they patronize.

Consumers demand the focus return to them

Have you thought about what the customer wants recently? If not, you will. Every business wants to please its customers, but few really understand what the customer wants. Today, social media enables consumers to tell everyone they know what exactly they want, and what they don't.

Every business can find out what the customer wants by talking to them directly in a social media conversation. Some companies fear that the social media conversation surrounding their products might be negative. But the conversation is happening *with or without* that company's consent and presence. Companies must develop relationships with people who actually use and care about your products, rather than creating focus groups or hiring survey takers.

Besides, if you aren't talking to your customers, who do you think is? Your competitors are already talking to them about what they like about your product vs. their own, and working to close the gap. Entrepreneurs who want to enter the market are talking to your customers and discovering what needs are not being met by your current products.

Join the conversation to figure out what your consumers are

already demanding, then work to determine how you can meet some of those needs.

Consumers control their own media

There was once a time when if you wanted to listen to music you turned on a radio. In exchange for hearing free music, you also had to listen to announcements, radio promotions, and advertising during the breaks. Now, if you want to listen to music, you use your mp3 player and listen to your own music, commercial free. If you want information, you can also listen to free podcasts based on your interests, not on the radio station's interests.

The same goes for TV. Instead of watching a show at the time the TV station has set, with commercials, you set your DVR and watch the show when you are free instead. You fast-forward through the commercials and only watch the good stuff, or you view shows online for free from sites like Hulu.

If you want news, you don't have to purchase the whole newspaper. You can go online and search for topics of interest. You also get the news from your friends on social networking sites, or from websites you frequent, all for free.

When consumers control their own media, they can filter your advertising right out of their lives. You have much less chance of getting eyeballs or ears on your message, unless the message is delivered by someone your consumer trusts, like a friend, colleague, or a valued news source. Businesses and individuals are using social media to share messages and build trust among a network of followers. Because consumers control their own media, businesses must gain trust among consumers or convince others **who already have trust** among consumers to spread the message.

Consumers want solutions, not products

As a small business, it's almost impossible to reach large groups of people one at a time on a personal level. Small businesses simply don't have the resources to develop one-to-one relationships with so many different people, especially when only a small portion will ever buy from them. And because small businesses have so few resources, it's also difficult to figure out who is interested in learning more about their products or services.

Also, consumers want something that *solves their problems*. Because there is so much free content, it takes a long time for a consumer to become comfortable with paying for a solution. Less than 13% of new web visitors purchase anything the first time they land on your site, and 37% of interested prospects take up to 3 months to actually make a purchase. Consumers want to get a feel for the company and think it over for a little while, before ever making a purchase.

From the company's perspective, you aren't looking for the "yes" commitment right away; all you are looking for is the first date with your consumer. Just like many guys start by asking for a girl's number, you can make the first step by developing the content your consumers want, to keep them around until they are ready to make the first purchase.

Social media is a good way to find the people who want to talk to you and your company. They will come to your business naturally because they are searching for solutions to their problems. Likewise, you can find the people you want to meet on social media, as long as you are participating. By developing personal relationships with these people, you can better create content they find relevant, which ultimately leads to purchases.

Consumers are blind to advertising

It is no secret that in the digital age, consumers are blind to advertising of all types. Several studies show the "banner blindness" effect, where internet users ignore anything that looks like an advertisement, even if it isn't. Also, studies show that pay-per-click advertising barely converts more often than organic search results.

This is good news for small businesses, because it levels the playing field between companies with large ad budgets and companies without. To break through the blindness, advertisers find that blended ads disguised as informational articles are the most effective way to reach consumers. That's why social media is one of the hottest trends in marketing right now: it reaches consumers with a message without advertising at them.

In the consumer's mind, advertising is a hard sell. It's a paid means to spread a message and there is little reason to pay attention. Social media is a soft sell; it allows the consumer to get to know you and your company. It allows a consumer to ease into the idea of purchasing your product or service.

So if businesses want to reach consumers with a message, social media is the perfect vehicle to facilitate the conversation.

Consumers distrust brands

To most people, social media is a sanctuary where they interact with their friends and their friends only. So what happens when brands enter? According to Forrester Research, only 16% of people trust corporate blogs and social networking profiles.

Another study shows that 91% of people who use social media claim they don't follow brands on Facebook or Twitter.

But is this true? Why do so many companies like Starbucks, Gatorade, and Threadless have millions of fans on these two networks then?

Most likely, people technically *are* following brands, but just don't realize it. That's because people who use social media don't follow companies, they follow *people*. For example, instead of following Zappos on Twitter, they follow Tony, the CEO of Zappos (who Twitters with the handle @zappos).

It's clear that consumers distrust brands, but they make exceptions when they like the people who represent the brand. In many cases, they don't even realize they are actually following a brand, because the person representing the brand is so engaging.

All of this means that small businesses need to put their best face forward and focus on reestablishing relationships with consumers, rather than relying on more traditional marketing tactics. When using social media, it's essential to put a *face* and *personality* to the brand.

Consumers trust recommendations from others

Did you know that while 78% of consumers trust peer recommendations, only 14% trust advertisements? And the closer the peer, the more trustworthy they become. Nielsen research claims that 90% of online consumers trust recommendations made by friends, while only 70% trust online product reviews from strangers. Recommendations from any source are considered unbiased, so consumers are much more likely to trust them over advertising.

The majority of recommendations are delivered online through social media. 34% of bloggers post opinions on products and brands, and (according to Razorfish) 71% of social media users share recommendations on products and services on social sites at least once every few months. Brands need their customers to recommend them to others in order to gain trust and make sales.

How sharing with social media helps businesses

Until now, I've focused on what the consumer wants, needs, and responds to. That's because it's the mindset that you must get into if you want to succeed at social media. Social media may be all about putting consumers first, but from a business perspective, there are also many reasons that sharing is a necessary means of dispersing a message.

Social media tools make it easy and cost effective

In the past, if you wanted to start a business, you first told all your friends. You got listed in the Yellow Pages and asked for referrals one at a time from each of your clients. You sent expensive direct mailings and hoped for a small conversion rate.

Now that people are using social media to find and share information, it's much easier for your business to get referrals online. In fact, websites like Amazon, Epinions, and Yelp are dedicated to sharing community-generated referrals for products and services. This means you not only have a larger reach due to lack of location barriers, but there is more opportunity for someone to share your message. Also, people have larger networks of weak ties online than in person, which means that every time someone shares information about your company, he or she has the potential to reach hundreds of people.

Social media lets others spread your message easily

As a single person or small team, you simply can't connect with every person you want to do business with. Your time is limited. When other people spread your message, you reach new networks of people (their networks) and their friends can **opt-in** to your company.

Word-of-mouth can spread both fast and slow, and there are advantages to both paths of dispersion. A fast spread means that you'll get major buzz for a few days, but then the buzz will drastically drop off due to over-exposure. The benefit is that your company can gain a great deal of publicity in a short period of time.

If your message doesn't get dispersed quickly, there is still advantage to the slow spread. There is a delay in sharing, which means that you can create a nice background buzz that lasts longer than one big push.

Social media makes word-of-mouth, buzz, and sharing easier to *track*

When someone shares something good or bad about your company over a phone call, a lunch conversation, or a dinner date, you have no way of knowing. You have no way of finding that person and sending a thank you card. You have no way of hearing exactly what he said to the other person and what finally convinced that person to try your product or service.

On social media, everything is traceable. You can find out who wrote about you, what exactly they said, how their network responded, and who became a customer because of it. You can find out how many times a customer was exposed to your brand before trying you out. You can test new ideas with a loyal fan base and a click of a button. You can search for information you forgot; you can create reports and demonstrate tangible results, and you can ultimately measure return on investment.

Some marketers, advertisers, and PR agencies harp on the intangible results of their efforts. But--hear this--if someone can't measure the results of social media efforts, they probably don't know what they are doing. Social media return on investment is covered in detail in later chapters of this book.

Summary

Sharing via social media is an essential part of your company's marketing mix for the following reasons:

- Consumers demand the focus return to them

- Consumers control their own media

- Consumers want solutions, not products

- Consumers are blind to advertising

- Consumers distrust brands

- Consumers trust peer recommendations

These trends are great for small businesses, because social media is easy to use, cost effective, viral, and easy to track.

Goals and Strategy

I hope that you are now thinking about why people will share your message using social media. Before we begin developing a message, however, we need to back up and talk about what we actually want to accomplish online with social media.

We need to talk about goals and strategy. Companies often skip this step because it's easier to focus on tactics and search for the secret sauce that just gets results. The truth is there is no secret sauce. The best way to get results is by *setting measurable goals* that align with your company's strategy, and *executing them*.

In this chapter, we will conduct a 360 degree assessment of your company and then talk about the types of marketing goals that social media can help you with. This exercise will also help you form an overall marketing strategy.

Your company

What are the company's main goals (outside of building an online presence or generating revenue)? The company's main goals must align with its social media goals.

How much time/money (per week or per month) can the company dedicate? How much time (per week or per month) can each individual employee dedicate, no matter what his or her position in the organization? By setting a realistic amount of time and resources the company can dedicate before looking at strategy, we bring real constraints to the forefront. This limits how many social media accounts your company will have and what you can do with each account. It also makes it easier to say "no." And remember, you aren't saying "no" forever; as the social media strategy grows, you can always add more people to your team.

What is the company's current web presence? What is the company currently doing online that is successful? What is the company currently doing online that is unsuccessful? Think of both websites and current social media accounts. This is your baseline. Your company should continue doing what is successful, cut what is unsuccessful, and add new ideas to test.

Your competition

List 3-5 main competitors. What social media accounts do they have online? What tools do they use? This is the group you will get your best ideas from, because you can either do the same thing or the complete opposite to compete. Get to know their followers, steal their followers, and set realistic goals for your own following.

With whom are your competitors interacting? These are some of the same people you need to have relationships with. These can be peers and influencers in the industry or potential customers.

What types of content are they producing? Can your company produce this content better, faster, cheaper, or in higher quantities? Who is your biggest enemy of the group? According to 37Signals cofounder Jason Fried, one way to motivate your company is by making an enemy. You should at least match what your competitors are doing online. Choose one competitor and make it your aim to win at social media.

What can you do to help customers understand the differences between you and your competition? Learn about your competitor's customers--find their pains--and teach them how things could be different if they used your service.

Your customer

Who is your customer? Find 5 actual customers who have an online presence. Note relevant demographic information, like location, age, gender, and B2B or B2C.

Where does your customer hang out online? What profiles do they have? What social networks do they use? These are the places you will find more potential customers, and the places you need to interact online.

What types of information does your customer currently consume? What social media styles do they consume (short text, long text, audio, video, etc.)? What types of information do they share? By creating content your customer likes to consume, you give them a reason to talk about you. You will also attract people with similar profiles naturally.

What types of information might your customer interested in? What questions does your customer have? Give them content they didn't ask for, that answers the questions they have.

Who is in your customer's network? How does your customer interact with individuals? How does your customer interact with other brands? How your customer interacts with others will teach you the *preferred method of sharing* for your consumer base. You can use this to better understand how word-of-mouth recommendations spread within your consumer base. How your customer interacts with other brands gives you constraints for how to reach out--what is good or bad--and allows you to build a model for how you can interact with customers the right way--their preferred way.

What are your customers already saying about you online? Don't forget, whether you join the conversation or not, your customers have already started it.

In marketing, it's said that profits are made at the intersection of where your company, competition, and customers are at.

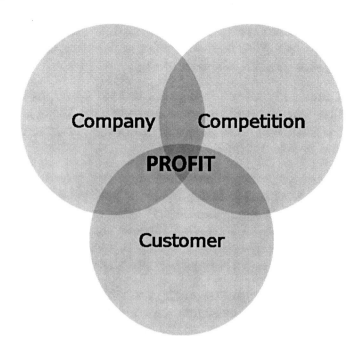

Before you make any major decisions about how you want to use social media, it is important to think carefully through these topics. Once you know the answers to these questions, you should have a fairly good idea of where your goals are headed.

The goals for using social media

Now that you have taken inventory of your company, competition, and customers, we are ready to talk about goals specifically for social media. In this section, I will describe seven goals for social media that cover about 90% of what companies are trying to accomplish.

Building brand awareness

The focus is on sheer impressions for your product or service. This goal is good for new brands, but doesn't make sense for a brand like Starbucks, of whom practically everyone is aware.

Establishing thought leadership

The focus is on gaining respect among peers in the community, not among consumers. When you gain respect among peers, you will also grow your consumer base. This goal is essential for freelancers, and can also be useful for startups.

Creating a sales pipeline

The focus is on qualifying prospective customers with free information and collecting their information. One health insurance company in Chicago has ten separate niche websites set up just to collect lead information that the sales team can use to generate more business.

Creating brand loyalty

The focus is on establishing relationships with current customers.

Customer support

The focus is on retaining current customers who have problems with your product. Every business knows that it's cheaper to keep a customer than to get a new one.

Human resources recruiting

The focus is on attracting and hiring external talent. Social media is replacing job boards because it's free and it's easier to qualify candidates based on skills and personality. This goal is important for larger companies that hire talent regularly.

Research and development

The focus is on product improvement and learning more about the needs and wants of consumers. This goal is important for companies that have a changing product (software, for example) but do not have a large budget for R&D.

You may have something more specific in mind for your company than the seven goals listed above, but this list is a great place to start. When I work with clients, I recommend starting with two or three goals only. Even if you only choose two or three goals to focus on, remember that none of these goals are mutually exclusive. Just having a presence on social media will help you accomplish all of these goals.

Here are some guidelines for choosing your two or three:

- Choose goals that emphasize what you are already doing that works

- Choose goals that ruthlessly cut anything you are doing that isn't working

- Choose goals that at least match what your direct competition is doing, but allow your company to do better

- Choose goals that make sense for the type of customer you are targeting and the type of content your customer is consuming and sharing

- Choose goals that fit within your company's budget and time constraints

Remember that you will use social media differently based on what your goals are. For example, if you are creating an eBook or free report to meet the thought leadership goal, you will make it downloadable for free so that it can be sampled and shared easily, and spread quickly. If you want to meet the sales pipeline goal, however, you will want to collect email addresses from individuals before they can get the download. That goal will decrease the number of people who received the eBook, but you would have a highly targeted lead list at the end of the day.

Every business wants to choose the right two or three goals, so let's look at each of them in more detail.

Brand awareness

Most companies could use more brand awareness. Use caution, though, when using social media for brand awareness, because traditional marketing and sales techniques do not work. Remember, brand awareness alone does not create sales.

The idea that "I just need to get in front of more people" is a complete lie perpetuated by the archaic tactics of the sales industry, specifically cold calling. You never need to just get your company in front of more people; what's important is getting in front of the **right** people who care about **your** products.

Also, market share on social media doesn't matter when you are a small company. Big numbers look pretty on paper, but

5000 Twitter followers are not going to help your company make payroll this month. The idea that market share is important is driven by larger, public companies who use market share as a metric to value their shareholdings. Unless you are taking in angel or VC funding (96% of small businesses are not), you will probably not need market share metrics.

If your goal is brand awareness, here are some questions you should consider:

- **Who are your most profitable market segments?** Focus on gaining brand awareness within those segments first.

- **If you are already hitting your most profitable segments, where can you find new audiences for your product?** Women entrepreneurs are probably interested in mom products. College-bound athletes also care about improving their study habits. Target niche segments with special offers to boost overall sales.

- **What other products can you offer that people could talk about?** If you own a coffee shop, maybe you could create a coffee table book to open new revenue streams.

- **What are your competitors doing to create brand awareness?** Shamelessly copy them, while learning from their mistakes and adding your own ideas to the mix.

- **What is the first impression you want to make on new consumers?** Brand awareness is all about creating a good first impression. It's not enough for people just to know you exist; you must also represent your company's personality, because that's how consumers will remember you once you get on their radar.

Thought leadership

Thought leadership is a good goal for companies with one or two dynamic founders or executives who have the charisma to also develop a following for their personal brands. These people may go to conferences, give speeches, and write books to gain extra press and publicity for the company.

Companies that demonstrate thought leadership almost always do it by association with a charismatic leader of the company. 37Signals is a company that demonstrates thought leadership in online software development through its founder, Jason Fried. Besides software, 37Signals offers books on software development and entrepreneurship, which helps build the company's credibility. Because its main customers are entrepreneurs and small businesses, thought leadership helps the company bring in new clients.

Thought leadership is not just for small businesses; it is a goal for companies of all sizes, from the solopreneur to the Fortune 100. Marissa Mayer is a VP at Google and serves as one of a small group of faces for the company, providing press interviews and speaking appearances for Google. If you have a one-person operation or a consultancy, thought leadership is an essential goal, because your business requires you to sell yourself as part of the product.

For your company to get recognized for thought leadership in its industry, you must do two things well: a) share insightful ideas and opinion about industry topics, and b) build relationships with other thought-leading companies in the industry.

If your goal is thought leadership, here are some questions you should consider:

- ***Is thought leadership essential for surviving in your industry?*** For most industries, it's not, and your company must be doing something truly remarkable to gain recognition. Efforts may be better spent targeting consumers rather than creating relationships with peers.

- **What companies do your employees look up to?** These are the companies you must take from a mentor relationship to a peer relationship. Unless you can do this, you will not reach your goal of thought leadership for your industry.

- **How will your company share ideas and build relationships?** It helps to have some contacts in place before attempting this goal.

- **Who should represent thought leadership at your company?** Founders, CEOs, or other executives are good choices. Choose someone who can be the face of the company and can establish the contacts needed to be successful.

Sales pipeline

Consider a model where your website visitors are prospects, your email subscribers are leads you are trying to convert to new customers, and your second lead list is a list of past customers who have bought from you before. Creating a sales pipeline is all about having a good lead list. The easiest way to create a lead list is to get people to **opt-in** for a free report, newsletter, or webinar. These free reports, eBooks, and webinars are called the bait.

Once you've created a lead list, you can give this lead list to your sales team and integrate the list into your current processes. By offering something of value, you can attract prospects to your sales pipeline and also integrate your new pipeline into your current CRM system.

If your goal is to build a sales lead list, here are some

questions you should consider:

- **How do your current customers buy? What channels do your current customers buy from? How do your competitor's customers buy?** This should give you insight into whether building a sales pipeline on the internet would be beneficial for your business.

- **What is the best channel to reach that customer? Is it social media?** If you already have a method of collecting leads, keep it running and try an online sales pipeline as an experiment. This method involves a great deal of testing on conversion rates. You will likely get fewer leads and the sales cycle for this pipeline may be longer (as it tends to be with social media).

- **How much does it cost me to reach the customer with this channel? How much is this particular customer worth?** In some cases, it might be useful to enact a small purchase price ($10 or so) to get more qualified leads.

You can get people to sign-up for your bribe by creating a high value informational product that solves a problem, and by offering it on a time-limited basis to create a sense of urgency.

Once you have leads, make sure you send them a welcome email and periodically send thank you notes and other useful information. All of this can be automated with email services like Aweber.

To collect email addresses, keep visitors on your site for as long as possible. You can use different pop-ups on various sections of your site to entice visitors to your free information products. Although pop-ups are annoying, they work! Just don't overdo it.

Brand loyalty

The success of our business often depends on the frequency at which we keep in touch with our customers. According to Jordan Media, "87% of businesses do not ask their customers for more business, yet your customers are 3 times more likely to do business with you." Sometimes social media is the best, most unobtrusive way to stay connected to customers, as opposed to constantly emailing or direct mailing them, because they can opt-in.

One easy way to create brand loyalty is a customer reward program. The program doesn't have to be anything fancy. It can be sharing coupons with certain social media accounts, emailing special promotions, or hosting giveaways for repeat customers. These programs also don't have to be expensive. You can offer products and services you already have as incentives.

If your goal is to build brand loyalty, here are some questions you should consider:

- **How can you introduce more switching costs to your current customers?** Creating higher switching costs is an easy way to keep customers from going to a competitor, but make sure you do it right! The most notorious industry for high switching costs is the cell phone industry, with exorbitant contract cancellation fees.

- **How can you keep current customers talking about your company?** Your most loyal customers are your fan base, and often are the best people to share their experiences with your company. Many companies offer brand loyalty incentives, such as a gift card when you refer a friend. By giving your loyal customers reasons to talk about you, you can create buzz and potentially gain new customers.

- **How can you manage discounts to avoid (in**

Buzz Tip: Brand loyalty is not just about keeping in touch!

The mortgage broker who helped my husband and I purchase our house kept us on his email and direct mailing lists for 2 years after the closing. He constantly sent us information about purchasing a home (which we had already done, and weren't planning to do again for at least five years) and refinancing (at higher interest rates than we currently had). One day, I finally emailed him and asked to be removed from the lists.

He asked if he had done something wrong. He hadn't done anything wrong when we worked with him on our first home loan; but *the information he was sending wasn't useful to us*, so I **opted out**.

You see, my mortgage broker wasn't thinking about anything more than keeping in touch with the customer so that the next time we needed a home loan, he could help us. Keeping in touch doesn't build brand loyalty on its own. Instead, he should have thought about what we, as new home owners, needed. If his newsletter had been about home decorating, or resolving disputes with neighbors, or changes in home insurance policies for my area, I would have gladly stayed on the list.

effect) lowering your prices? When companies contin-uously give coupons to their loyal customers, it effective-ly lowers the price of the product. One retail chain in St. Louis put coupons for 15% off in the weekend paper, every single weekend. Their customers became accustomed to discounts, and stopped purchasing anything at full price! If you plan to use discounts to create brand loyalty, make sure your promotions are irregular and unpredictable.

Customer support

Customer contact is crucial; but what happens if your cus-tomers are not contacting you? It does not mean they are happy with your services!

When it comes to customer support, companies wait for their customers to contact them with issues. But in most cases, customers accept when they have an issue as long as it is resolved quickly and easily. Social media can help custom-ers and companies by providing an easy way for custom-ers to voice their issues (without having to call and wait on the phone for an hour) and receive a response quickly (fast-er than a phone call or email). The faster you respond, the more your customers feel you care about them.

If your goal is to manage customer support, here are some questions you should consider:

* **Will you use social media to answer support tickets or simply filter them?** Passive customer sup-port consists of monitoring mentions of your product or company on social media, while active customer support would be actually handling and resolving tickets on social media. Whichever you choose, know that customers may ask support questions via social media whether your goal is customer support or not. Essentially, every company on social media deals with passive customer support on some level.

- ***How can you decrease the need for repeat work?***
Some companies have a knowledge database, but smaller businesses often do okay with a detailed FAQ (Frequently Asked Questions) list. You could set up a FAQ list based on questions you get through social media, and then post the link on your social media profile.

Recruiting

Some companies may want to use social media for recruiting purposes. This could be either hiring talent for a company or recruiting students for private schools or colleges and universities. Social media is especially useful for the recruiting needs of schools, Fortune 500 companies, or high-growth companies who hire at least 3 new people per week. For small companies, it is probably not as useful to set up accounts specifically for recruiting.

If your goal is to recruit, here are some questions you should consider:

- ***Should your company have separate social media accounts for recruiting?*** Only you can decide. Recruiting content includes pictures of the company, awards, and information about the company's culture. All of these are also appropriate for brand building goals, so there is no right answer.

- ***What communities do our targets frequent?*** Check out targeted skills communities (for example, a PHP developer community if you are looking for programmers) and also look at competitor communities. To actively search for candidates, LinkedIn and niche business or professional sites are useful.

Research and development

Research and development is one area where most small businesses do not spend nearly enough time. Social media makes it easier for companies to do cost-effective research, which can help the company perfect its products and services, and create new opportunities for products.

There are many ways that you can use social media for R&D, including creating a feedback form on your website, crafting a survey and sending it out to your social media contacts, tracking the digital footprint your visitors leave on your website, or polling your social media contacts about new product offerings.

If your goal is to use social media to conduct R&D, here are some questions you should consider:

- *How will you collect data? How will you interpret it?* This will be discussed at length in the measurement section of this book.

- *What are you developing?* Most companies are either trying to make improvements to their current products or create new products or services. Improvements to current products can be much easier to research using social media because consumers already have a prototype to reference.

- *Does your company need qualitative or quantitative data?* If you need qualitative data, you can do passive research by looking at what consumers like and talk about and who they interact with on social media. If you need quantitative data, you will likely just use social media as a means to get participation on surveys and in focus groups.

Summary

In this chapter, we completed a 360 degree assessment of your company which took a look at your company, competitors, and customers and their online interaction.

We also talked about seven goals in social media:

- Brand Awareness

- Thought Leadership

- Sales Pipeline

- Brand Loyalty

- Customer Support

- Recruiting

- Research and Development

Finally, we went over guidelines for choosing each goal as a potential priority for your business.

Choose Your Social Media Channels

To promote the movie Firewall, Pod Digital Design agency wanted to target 16-25 year old males online. Rather than trying to attract an audience to the movie, Pod found media sites that were already engaging this demographic well. They stumbled on a genre of games that were popular on these sites, called "Escape from the Room" games.

To win one of these games, players would have to search for clues to find the one exit. Several scenes from the Firewall movie fit in well with the premise of this type of game, and Pod realized they could create Inside the Firewall, a version of the "Escape from the Room" games that engaged their target demographic in the movie's plot. They could then push Inside the Firewall on sites where young males were already playing these types of games.

The campaign was successful, with nearly half a million games played and a 38% click through rate to the movie trailer. The key to the game's success was twofold – Pod found the movie's audience online first, then created content that both tied into the movie promotion and was already a hit with the audience.

Likewise, you too must find your audience online. Now that you have social media goals, you must align those goals with the best distribution channel for your content. This is how you create a strategy that makes sense for your company.

Many people use every social media account they can just because that's what an article or a consultant tells them to do. But that is a mistake. You should consider your goals, your time and resource commitments, and your need for each and every tool before trying to build a presence on it. You should also consider what assets your business already has that will help you build a successful presence on each social media site you're interested in.

When choosing between social networks, consider the size and popularity of the site, the reach the site has, the demographics of each site, and topics that do best on each site.

Remember, your success is based on using social media the way it will work best for your business. Tools and trends come and go; technology changes at snap of a finger. The most successful company keeps its goals foremost as it evaluates its social media activity.

In this chapter, we will cover the various categories of social media and how people are using them to share content. Within each category, you can see whether the category makes sense for your goals, and which tools within the category target the demographics you want. You will also learn what types of content work best for which distribution channels, and the benefits and disadvantages of each social media tool.

Blogs

Currently, blogs are the best way to share big ideas that need a lot of explanation. In many cases, the most insight comes not from the blog post itself, but from the conversations that take place in the comments section. The most successful blogs, like TechCrunch or Huffington Post, are in the news or content development business. If you are going to blog well, the content must be highly original and solve problems--answering questions that people are searching the internet for.

The types of content that are shared with blog posts are any form of longer content (especially opinions, research findings, and ideas), pictures, and video. People share blog posts by using permanent links or a shortened link. These links are embedded within articles, other blog posts or the comments sections of other blog posts, and shared on social networks, bookmarking sites, and via email.

Blogs are one of the highest maintenance forms of social media. If your goal is thought leadership, blogging is essential. They are also helpful for other goals like brand awareness, brand loyalty, and recruiting.

Benefits - Blogs are the best way to optimize a website for search engines and a good opportunity to promote content and ideas.

Downsides - Blogs require a long-term investment because they take a lot of work to maintain.

Tools to optimize and integrate - As a company, there is no substitute for a self-hosted blog. You can find free blog software from Wordpress.org, or Typepad.org. There are many free plugins from Wordpress.org. RSS Feeds are also an essential part of optimizing and sharing with blogs.

Buzz tip: Best wordpress.org plugins for sharing

While there are many blog software options, my rec-ommendation is always Wordpress. It is widely used to run blogs of all sizes and has a large technical sup-port community that creates downloadable add-ons called plugins. Check out these Wordpress plugin recommendations:

- AddtoAny Button

- Share on Facebook

- Share Google Reader picks

Download at: http://wordpress.org/extend/plugins

Miniblogs

The best content for this format includes anything too short for a blog post and too long for a tweet. Photos, videos, quotes, short blog posts, news clips, and charts work well on miniblogs. People use miniblogs to share ideas, opinion, links, and humorous items they find on the web.

Viral marketing comes into play when people in the origina-tor's network re-blog, give thumbs up, or comment on the post. Each post also has a unique URL and can be shared on social networks or microblog sites.

Miniblogs don't require as much time as blogs and are a good substitute for social media users who want to share content rather than create it. The difference between miniblogs and regular blogs is the tools that allow people to share content quickly and easily.

Miniblogs work well for almost every goal. They are less useful than blogs when it comes to thought leadership and would not be a great way to handle customer support, but the format is fluid enough to handle many different types of medium-sized content that you would not typically see in blog posts, like simple polls and surveys.

Benefits - Sharing via miniblog is easy, social capabilities are built-in, and you can create content quickly. Also, most miniblog services allow you to host your blog from your own domain name.

Downsides - Miniblogs are less flexible than regular blogs for creating content, and there is no popular open source software for creating a miniblog on your own site (you must use traditional blogging software). This means miniblogs are harder to customize.

Two major players in the miniblog space right now are Tumblr and Posterous. Tumblr was created primarily to share content like short posts, quotes, chats, pictures, and video quickly and easily through the web. While Posterous also has an interface for posting via the web, the service is focused on posting content on the go, from your email tool, and then pushing the content to all your social network sites.

Tumblr

3-4 million unique visitors per month. Most users are in the US, Japan, Europe, and Canada. The most popular topics are humor, politics, technology, adult, and fashion.

Posterous

1 million unique visitors per month. Most users are in the US, Canada, or Europe, and the demographics lean towards middle-aged men with diverse ethnicities. The most popular topics are humor, politics, science, news, and academics.

Microblogging/messaging sites

People cannot share very much content in the 140 – 160 characters that microblogging and messaging sites offer. Therefore, the most shared information on these sites is links to longer content on other social media sites or blogs. On microblogging sites, attribution to the originator of the message is an important element of sharing. For example, Twitter uses two letters – "RT" (for "re-tweet") – followed by the originator's handle to give attribution when sharing. Learn the syntax for giving attribution on each microblogging site so you can share correctly.

When using microblogging to gain clients, make sure you are not using the service as a broadcasting tool. Instead, use it as an interactive tool, and share your expertise while also conversing with others. Many of your updates will be replies to other people on the network. This is expected and will boost your profile and status, showing that as a company, you are interested in creating real relationships with consumers.

Maintenance for microblogging sites is low to medium, depending on how much time you want to invest. On most microblogging sites, you can automatically share RSS feeds with your stream of followers, which helps cut down on the maintenance time.

Benefits - Interaction is high and sharing is easy on these sites. Your company can find a large audience in a short time, with less maintenance than several other types of social media.

Downsides - The brevity of this medium is limiting. Sharing links is easy, but those links must go to somewhere, meaning that your company will not have much luck using microblogging without combining it with other social networking sites.

Twitter

28 million unique visitors per month. Nearly half of the users in the US are between the ages of 18-35. The most popular topics are fashion/cosmetics, teens, news, humor, and music.

Plurk

A quarter of a million unique visitors per month. Over half of the users are between the ages of 18-34, and half of the users make less than $30k per year. Users of this tool like to talk about food, universities, technology, online trading, and politics.

Identi.ca

100,000 unique visitors per month. Users are middle-aged male in the middle income range.

Yammer

90,000 unique visitors per month. Yammer is a professional site; it hosts closed networks and aims at becoming the corporate version of Twitter.

Jaiku

40,000 unique visitors per month. The site caters to the older middle-income crowd with no kids under 12 in the house.

Pownce

 15,000 unique visitors per month. The users on the network lean heavily male, with over half between the ages of 35-49. The site also has mostly college-educated users, with 26% also holding masters degrees or above.

Networks: social, professional, and special interest sites

There are networks for just about every topic imaginable, but networks generally fall into three categories: social, professional, or special interest.

The types of content shared on such networks include photos, audio, video, links, status updates, polls, surveys, and just about everything else you can of. Often, networks have their own version of several others types of social media sites. For example, Facebook has built-in videos, photo albums, chat features, events, and a marketplace for listings, in addition to the purely social aspect with profiles.

Individuals share on networks by creating a profile, and companies share on networks by creating groups or pages for their products, services, or company brand. Maintenance for all of these networks requires medium effort, depending on how involved you want to be.

On social networks, people share humorous, silly, or interesting content of all types with their close network of friends. Most people's social networks consist of family, friends, and school/organization contacts. Social networks are useful for reaching consumers, and work well if your goals are brand awareness, brand loyalty, or R&D.

On professional networks, people share projects they are working on, slide presentations, resume and cover letter information, achievements, job opportunities, and professional advice. These networks are a must if your goal is recruiting or thought leadership, and can also be helpful if your customers are other businesses or your products appeal to business professionals.

When looking for networks to join, you should also look for special interest networks. For example, if you are an author, there are niche networking sites where book lovers hang out, like GoodReads and LibraryThing. You can also search Ning.com, which is a site that hosts user-generated special interest networks.

Benefits - Networks are targeted and you can often find groups of people who are already interested in your industry or product.

Downsides - Networks are often closed to search engines and many people put privacy locks on their profiles to avoid exposing personal information to strangers.

Social networks

Facebook

300 million users. About 70% of users are between the ages of 13-34. Users on the network have above-average incomes. The most popular topics are fashion/cosmetics, teens, news, parenting, and humor.

MySpace

150 million users. About 70% of users are between the ages of 13-34. Users on the network have below-average incomes and over half do not have a college degree. The most popular topics are music, teens, humor, gaming, and parenting.

Tagged

40 million users. Users lean towards middle-aged female with kids 13-17 in the house. Over 70% of the users make less than $60k per year. The most popular topics are humor, teens, music, education, and horoscopes.

Classmates

40 million users. The site appeals to an older demographic of users who want to reconnect with past classmates from

kindergarten through college or even the military.

Bebo

31 million users. The main demographic is teens, with about 60% being female. The most popular topics are humor, music, gaming, education, and fashion.

Professional networks

LinkedIn

50 million users. This site is popular in the US. The demographics are middle-aged men and women who are more affluent, often holding graduate or post-graduate degrees. The most popular topics are networking, career growth, business, and job searching.

Plaxo

20 million users. Users on the site are older affluent men and women. There are more women than men on this site. The most popular topics are politics, genealogy, nature, universities, and technology.

Xing

8 million users. This site is popular in Europe. Users on the site are middle-aged men and women with average incomes. There are more men than women on this site. Popular topics include politics, genealogy, nature, universities, and technology.

Ecademy

Users on the site are affluent middle-aged men and women. There are more men than women on this site. The most popular topics are nature, politics, career resources, technology, nonprofit, and regional/local news.

Brazen Careerist

15,000 users. Users on this site are college-educated with split demographics between 18-35 year olds and 50+ year olds. The most popular topics are Gen Y, careers, social media, and news.

Special interest networks

Ning

Over 1 million social networks created. Ning is a website where anyone can host a social network based on their interests and passions. The most popular topics are humor, teens, fashion, nature, gaming, and music.

Case Study: Creating brand loyalty with a special interest network

American Skiing Company wanted to improve the customer's experience with the "All for One" multi-resort season pass. ASC created a special interest network just for the season pass holders and encouraged them to network with each other and create videos, photos, and blog posts about their vacations. By creating a two-way dialogue, ASC was able to listen to customer complaints and improve the overall experience for season pass holders.

The network had nearly 4,000 members with 44% active each month. Participants helped spread the word about their season pass experiences and also became loyal fans of ASC.

Bookmarking sites

Bookmarks are one of the easiest ways to get your articles and your information noticed.

People share on social bookmarking sites by posting links that are tagged or reviewed. The only content you can share through these sites is links to other content. Most bookmarking sites have a system for gaining votes so that the best (most popular) links bubble to the top. The more votes your submitted content gets, the more you rise in influence on the social bookmarking site. (Note that your submitted content does not have to be your own.) Users can also comment on links or share them with their friends on the site, which helps their links rise in popularity.

You can also share your bookmarks anywhere on the web using the feed attached to your profile. Sharing your bookmarks is a good way to become a filter of news and information for your consumers.

Bookmarking sites require only a few minutes of your time and are well worth the effort. Social bookmarking is good for any goals except customer support. Maintenance is low for bookmarking sites as long as you only focus your efforts on one or two that produce the best results for you.

Benefits - Social bookmarking is a fast way to share and keep a record of links on the internet. The tagging and categorizing systems found on most of these sites make it easy to find relevant links related to your industry or product.

Downsides - You can only share a limited amount of content, you are sometimes penalized for submitting your own content, and you usually need a strong network on the site to earn heavy traffic numbers. Also, it's often not that useful for a company to build a company profile, unless they have a corresponding blog where they can post the links. Bookmarking is more useful for individuals who are researching blog post or article topics.

Digg

44 million unique visitors per month. Users on this site are primarily young adult males with a college education. The most popular topics are science, humor, politics, technology, news, and cars.

StumbleUpon

5 million unique visitors per month. Users on this site are older men and women. The most popular topics are humor, technology, fashion, politics, news, and nonprofit.

Reddit

5 million unique visitors per month. Users on this site are young adults – both male and female. The most popular topics are nature, politics, technology, news, and nonprofit.

Delicious

2 million unique visitors per month. Users on this site are middle-aged men and women. The most popular topics are politics, humor, technology, commerce, and music.

Mixx

1 million unique visitors per month, with similar demographics to Digg. Popular topics include science, humor, politics, technology, media, and news.

You can also get a list of niche social bookmarking sites at:

http://searchenginejournal.com/125-social-bookmarking-sites-importance-of-user-generated-tags-votes-and-links/6066

Photo-sharing sites

Images are perfect for sharing because they are visual and they often include people or events. Users share by tagging people in the images; others use images to jazz up a website or a blog post. For events, if you have a large group of people to share the images, you can get the word out about the event after it has already happened. It's marketing for the next event.

You can also tag and categorize images the same way you tag and categorize links. Others can find your images through search engines and search functionality on each site when they search for keywords that relate to your tags or categories.

The types of content shared via this format include images, artwork, logos, charts and graphs, graphics, and images of products.

Photo-sharing sites are low maintenance--all you have to do is upload your images and add a few tags of description.

Benefits - If you optimize your images for search engines, they can be found easily because there is much less competition. You can also incorporate images into many other different types of media, like blog posts and slideshows, to make the content more visually stimulating. Adding images to your site is a great way to drive traffic. It's also a good way to add interest.

Downsides - The downside to using images is that it is harder to convey a specific message, and that message is open to interpretation. Images are rarely vehicles for a full message, but can help supplement a message.

Facebook Photos

35 million unique visitors per month. About 70% of users

are between the ages of 13-34. Users on the network have above-average incomes. The most popular topics are fashion/cosmetics, teens, news, parenting, and humor.

Flickr

30 million unique visitors per month. 70% of users are between the ages of 18-49. The most popular topics are humor, nature, technology, and fashion.

Photobucket

23 million unique visitors per month. The main demographic is teens, with over 70% of users under 35 years old. The most popular topics are humor, teens, gaming, music, and fashion.

Webshots

5 million unique visitors per month. About 60% of users are above 35 years old. The most popular topics are humor, cars, technology, nature, universities, and pets.

Audio/radio networks

Podcasting is a great way to bring your brand to life and connect with your target audience. With a well-developed podcast, your company has the opportunity to give people genuine face time (with a real person--you perhaps) and recruit new clients.

Unlike traditional radio, where the radio host or DJ dictates what the listener will hear, podcasting puts the subscriber in control. The subscriber can hear your program anytime with an MP3 player.

Podcast content includes talk shows, language tutorials, books, and interviews, to name but a few. People share

Podcast Directory Submissions

A Podcast Like That - http://www.podcastlikethat.com/

AllPodcasts - http://www.allpodcasts.com/PingAll/Default.aspx

AmigoFish - http://www.amigofish.com/catcher/podcast/submit

Blubrry - http://www.blubrry.com/createaccount.php

Canada Podcast - http://canada.podcast.com/home.php

Digital Podcast - http://www.digitalpodcast.com/login.php?f=1&b=add_anywhere.php%3Fcat%3D1

Education Podcast Network - http://epnweb.org/index.php?view_mode=suggest

Feedshark - http://feedshark.brainbliss.com/

Fluctu8 - http://www.fluctu8.com/add-podcast.php

FMG Women's Network - http://www.womeninpodcasting.com/addcast.html

GigaDial - http://www.gigadial.net/public/find-by-podcaster

Godcast1000 - http://www.godcast1000.com/

Government Central - http://www.government-central.com/submitrss.php

iBiz Radio - http://www.ibizradio.com/add.html

Idiotvox - http://www.idiotvox.com/index.php?spid=7

iTunes - http://www.apple.com/itunes/podcasts/

Plazoo - http://www.plazoo.com/en/addrss.asp

Penguin Radio - http://www.podcastdirectory.com/ add/

Pluggd - http://www.pluggd.tv/

Podblaze - http://www.podblaze.com/directory_ submit.php

Podcast Alley - http://www.podcastalley.com/add_a_ podcast.php

Podcast Blaster - http://www.podcastblaster.com/ directory/add-podcast/

Podcast Pickle - http://www.podcastpickle.com/

Podcasting Station - http://www.podcasting-station. com/submitrss.php

Podfeed - http://www.podfeed.net/add_podcast.asp

Podlounge - http://www.thepodlounge.com.au/ add_podcast

Political Feeds - http://www.political-humor.net/ submitrss.php

RSS Network - http://www.rss-network.com/ submitrss.php

Sports Feeds - http://www.sports-feeds.com/ submitrss.php

Syndic8 - http://www.syndic8.com/suggest. php?Mode=site

podcasts using RSS feeds, iTunes, other podcast directories, and by embedding them in posts or on websites. If your company works in the music industry, you can use niche music sites like Pandora, which create radio stations for users based on artists they like.

To get the podcast picked up on search engines, you can upload the transcript to your website along with the podcast. You can also use the text of the transcript to promote your podcast. Quote a guest who said something interesting, use segments for comments, and generally publicize your podcast by using bits of the transcripts on social networks.

Podcasting takes some time to plan episodes, record, and edit, but the tools are free. You can use free editing software like Audacity, or use Audio Acrobat to record unedited segments. Podcasts are good for goals of thought leadership, brand awareness, sales pipeline, and brand loyalty.

Benefits - Compared to blogging, podcasting is less popular which means there is less competition to create a memorable podcast. Podcasts also take less time to create than long articles or blog posts.

Downsides - Podcasts are not search-engine friendly, and they are tougher to edit than a blog post or article.

You can host your podcast on your own site, but most people find podcasts through podcast directories. Get your podcast listed in every directory you can because it's free and a relatively easy way to gain more listeners.

Video networks

Video networks have videos of widely varying quality levels, from amateur unscripted posts to professional made-for-MTV music videos. These videos can be humorous, goofy, informative, or purely commercial.

Anyone can email or embed videos or share the permanent links on other social media sites, including their blogs. You can also share by letting others subscribe to your channel. Videos are grouped into categories and users can often rate and comment on the videos as a way to vote for them. The ratings combined with views pushes the video to the front page of the site.

Videos require a medium level of maintenance, depending on how you use them. It takes longer to put together a better video that has the chance to go viral, but it does not take much time to put together an impromptu or unedited video. Videos can be used for goals like brand awareness, thought leadership, brand loyalty, and recruiting.

Benefits - You can connect with your audience very easily because they can see and hear you. With a charismatic personality, you can establish credibility easily.

Downsides - Video production is time consuming and may require tech-savvy, especially if you plan to edit the material heavily.

YouTube

86 million unique visitors per month. Teens are heavy users of this site, with roughly 60% of the users under 35 years old. The most popular topics are humor, teens, music, politics, and gaming.

SlideShare

23 million unique visitors per month. While not strictly a video network, SlideShare gives business users the ability to upload slides, documents, and other files to share on the network. Users can also add a timed audio track to the slides for an interactive feel similar to video. Business professionals are the main users of this site, with over 90% of users above 18 years old.

Metacafe

6 million unique visitors per month. The demographic is young adults, though over half of the users do not hold a college degree. There are more men than women on this site. The most popular topics are humor, adult, commerce, music, and technology.

Veoh

4 million unique visitors per month. Over half of the users do not hold a college degree, and there are more men than women on this site. The most popular topics are humor, teens, commerce, music, and gaming.

Vimeo

3 million unique visitors per month. It's difficult to find demographic information on this site, but the most popular topics are politics, humor, nature, technology, and nonprofit.

Viddler

1 million unique visitors per month. The primary audience is young adults with slightly more men than women using the site. The most popular topics are humor, politics, technology, home and gardening, and news.

Ecommerce and review sites

If you have a product or a location-based business, ecommerce and review sites are an essential part of your social media strategy. Most ecommerce sites allow you to list your products for a nominal fee, meaning the cost of adding your products to each site is very little compared to other potential distribution channels.

Recommendations play a huge role in Ecommerce sites.

Recommendations are some of the strongest forms of advertisement businesses have to convince consumers to try their products or services. According to Word of Mouth Marketing Association (WOMMA), "Studies show that two-thirds of all economic activity is influence by customer recommendations." The content shared on review sites includes general business information (like address, hours, and services) or product information and customer's experiences and opinion. The opinions of your customers as recorded on such sites can play a large role in whether a new customer will do business with you.

Companies can create business profiles on review sites and interact with their reviewers by sending thank you notes or even requesting reviews from top reviewers. The time it takes to maintain these profiles is low compared to the payoffs.

In general, allowing customers to share opinions on the internet helps businesses spread the word. According to popular review site Yelp, 32% of all reviews on their website are 5 star reviews. 35% are four stars, 18% are 3 stars, 8% are 2 stars, and 7% are 1 star reviews. That means if you ask your customers for a review, you have a good chance of helping your brand rather than harming it.

Benefits - Everything sounds better coming from your customer. A good review is worth much more than any advertising you could do and people use review sites to make important purchase decisions.

Downsides - You have no control over how people review your product, so you have to be willing to accept the bad with the good. If you have a good product, there should be nothing to worry about!

EBay

77 million unique visitors per month. Users are primarily

Case Study: Bath and Body Works email marketing campaign

Bath and Body Works sent out an email marketing campaign containing customer review content, and compared the results to its normal campaigns. The results from website visitors (a website visitor defined as someone who clicked to the website from the email campaign) were:

- 2.36% lower bounce rate

- 7.48% more page views

- 13.6% higher average session length

- 11.46% more sales

- an average order value 10.04% higher

Customer reviews matter! Use your customer reviews everywhere – they are your best form of advertising.

affluent middle-aged men and women. The most popular items sold relate to cars, hobbies, collectibles, sports, and home.

Amazon

70 million unique visitors per month. Users are primarily affluent middle-aged men and women. The most popular items sold relate to books, department stores, home, consumer electronics, and fashion/cosmetics.

Yelp

32 million unique visitors per month. Although this website

doesn't sell products, it is one of the largest review sites around. Users are primarily very affluent urban young adults, with over 30% making over $100,000. The most popular reviews relate to fashion, travel, home furnishings, fragrances, and restaurants.

Etsy

5 million unique visitors per month. The site allows users to list and sell handmade products. Users are primarily less affluent young adult women. The most popular items sold relate to hobbies, family, home décor, fragrances, and jewelry.

Information Hubs

People use information hubs to create longer, in-depth, magazine-style articles about single topics. These hubs serve as online encyclopedias that anyone can contribute to. Sharing of knowledge is encouraged through profit-sharing or through fan loyalty. The site also lends credibility to the author, and gives the author's content a higher page rank on search engines. While each hub has its own monetization scheme (and some do not share profits with content creators at all), all hubs work to preserve the integrity of the site content.

You can share any type of content on hub sites, but this type of media is best for the goals of thought leadership and brand awareness. You can establish thought leadership by publishing important articles about your industry, and you can create brand awareness by publishing factual information about your product, your company, or your executive team.

Benefits - Information hubs are viewed as a source of credibility, are easily found in search engines, and are cited in as research resources.

Downsides - In some cases, you do not get credit,

ownership, and/or payment for the content you create.

Hubpages

6 million unique visitors per month. Users are less affluent men and women with college degrees. Popular topics include fashion, parenting, nature, humor, and home and gardening.

Wikipedia

4 million unique visitors per month. Users are teens with over 70% of users under 35 years old. Popular topics include humor, gaming, news, fashion, technology, and politics.

Squidoo

1.5 million unique visitors per month. Users are less affluent middle-aged men and women with college degrees. Popular topics include fashion, humor, parenting, nature, children's education.

Google Knol

200,000 unique visitors per month. Users are middle-aged affluent men and women with college degrees. Popular topics include nature, universities, technology, kids, and nonprofit.

Answer sites

You can use user-generated questions to inspire blog posts and understand what people are searching for that they can't find an answer to with just search engines. The treasure here is understanding what pains consumers have. You can then create products and services that resolve those pains.

People share information on answer sites because it helps establish credibility in an industry or areas of expertise. You can information and links, get votes for being helpful, become the best answer (chosen by person asking the question) and have your profile found search engines.

You can also ask questions to do ad hoc consumer research and generate feedback.

Answer sites require medium to high maintenance. It takes time to find questions in your industry and answer them. Because you don't start the conversation, you may need to do some research or digging to answer the question well.

Benefits - Easy and best way to establish expertise for thought leadership. Good way to do ad hoc R&D if used properly.

Downsides - There are less benefits if your answer isn't chosen or voted on, because it doesn't appear at the top. You must invest the time if you want your answers to be the highest quality and appear at the top.

Yahoo! Answers

30 million unique visitors per month. Users are male and female with the largest groups between the ages of 18-49. The most popular topics are parenting, fashion, nature, humor, and home and gardening.

LinkedIn Answers

It's difficult to get traffic or demographics information on this answer site within a social networking site; however, topics are grouped by both business function and industry.

Event sites

People use event sites to share what events they are going to, especially with networking events or webinars where they could meet with someone in their network.

The types of content shared on event sites include virtual events like webinars, and in-person events like parties, networking events, lectures, and seminars.

Many event sites are now adding Facebook and Twitter sharing tools so people can tell their networks they are attending your events.

Benefits - No matter why you are holding the event, people have a reason to share their attendance with others. People will want to share with their online networks to see if anyone else they know is attending the event. The virality is built in.

Downsides - If your product or service is not one which you can hold events for, you won't find much to do on event sites.

Evite

9 million unique visitors per month. Users are middle-aged affluent men and women, with more women than men on the site. The most popular types of events advertised on Evite are bridal events, home furnishing events, baby shower events, travel events, and sports events.

Meetup

3 million unique visitors per month. Users are middle-aged affluent men and women, with more women than men on the site. The most popular types of events advertised deal with politics, nature, nonprofit, and regional or local news.

Eventbrite

1 million unique visitors per month. Users are middle-aged affluent men and women, with more women than men on the site. The most popular types of events advertised deal with politics, religion, travel, home décor, news, and nonprofit.

Use this list

To use this list, consider which categories make the most sense for your company, and then use demographic and topical information to decide which platform has a high concentration of your targeted audience. Also consider the size of the network overall – a large site that does not target your audience specifically may still be better than a small site that does target your audience. In some cases, it's beneficial to use both sites.

All information for various social media sites was collected from Quantcast.com and Compete.com. The information is meant for filtering purposes only, to give you and your company some clear guidelines for shaping a social media strategy and choosing accounts. Links and data change, move, or get removed so for the most up-to-date information (or more information) on these social media sites, search for the site on the free versions of Compete.com and Quantcast. com.

Before creating a campaign for any of these sites, spend time on each site to understand how people converse and share. Understanding the natural flow of sharing for every site is essential to spreading your message with social pollination.

Summary

Choose social media tools from the categories that align with your company's goals. The categories are:

- Blogs

- Miniblogs

- Microblogs

- Social, Professional, and Special Interest Networks

- Bookmarking Sites

- Photo-Sharing Sites

- Podcasts

- Video Networks

- Ecommerce and Review Sites

- Information Hubs

- Answer Sites

- Event Sites

By investing in just a few highly targeted social media profiles, your company can engage its audience and budget effort and resources better.

Learn more

Add these three blogs to your feed reader to learn more about the tools of social media:

TechCrunch (http://techcrunch.com) - TechCrunch is the leading source for startup and acquisition information. Many new social media tools come from startups, so TechCrunch covers these new technologies.

Mashable (http://mashable.com) - Mashable is the #1 social media blog. It covers research, trends, and tools in social media.

ReadWriteWeb (http://readwriteweb.com) - ReadWrite Web is about web products and trends. It covers social media and other topics in web technology.

Build Your Platform

At 4 years old, there was nothing I wanted more than a subscription to the Disney Channel.

Every once in awhile, Disney would give away a free week of its channel, and would broadcast a room full of operators who were standing by to sign you up. The channel operated under this premium subscription model for 13 years, and reached about 8 million homes in the late '90s.

Then, the Disney Channel moved from a premium channel to free with an extended cable package in 1997. The channel, however, did not adopt the traditional advertising model most cable networks have. Instead, it used its channel as a platform for Disney promotions.

The Disney Channel is a marketing machine. Every piece of content the Disney Channel puts out does one thing: sells more merchandise, more movies, more music, and more concerts. Shows like Hannah Montana, Sonny with a Chance, and the High School Musical movies have all been created to feed Disney's music label, Hollywood Records, and Disney's merchandising division, which delivers mass-market product lines branded with the stars of Disney Channel Original Series and Movies. According to Conde Nast Portfolio, the Disney Channel has gained millions of new viewers *every month* for the last five years as a result of its strategy.

Building a platform is one of the most important things you can do for your company, right now. Because of the internet, simply selling content is no longer a good business model. To add to the confusion, developing a message for social media is different from developing a message for an ad campaign, because anyone who sees the message is opting in to your message rather than tuning it out. They are following you, subscribing to you, or becoming friends with you – and they are worth far more than someone who just sees your advertisement.

In fact, you may have to develop messages that do not appear to further your goals but *actually* do, simply because they give people a reason to opt-in. You can think of this as part of the lead generation process. It is worth getting the opt-in because you will not be considered to be spamming or cold calling. You are targeting people who want to be reached by you.

You see, the way to sell products and services online is by giving away as much or more than you sell, so you can get an opt-in. That's how you get more customers. This does not mean you shouldn't sell content at all. It means you have to offer a lot of free content to build a platform, which then enables you to sell more premium content.

Radiohead realized this in 2007 when they released their album, *In Rainbows*, online – giving fans the choice to download for free or give a donation. Despite giving the music away for free, two-thirds of people still paid an average CD price and the sales of their physical album were also stronger than their previous album.

Really, this is a fascinating concept: free content actually **increases** sales for paid content. This is not true just for industries that sell content – it's also true for industries that sell pizza or auto parts, if you look closely.

It's a simple formula: **Content = Customers**.

The more quality content you create for free, the more content you can sell.

Build a platform

To build a platform, you have to first build two pillars – a relationship pillar, and a content pillar. Then, you must optimize each for social pollination.

The relationship pillar

- **Build trust.** When it comes to information, ideas, and products, most are free online. Why should someone trust you over anyone else? It's not enough to be friendly with your customers, share your tips, or respond to their emails; you must actually *become friends* with them. Trust comes from creating friendships with real people.

- **Connect with others.** Most of the messaging a person receives is from his or her network. It's essential for companies to learn to network with its customers.

- **Create dialogue.** At one time, companies had a monologue with its customers. Companies put out television commercials or print ads about its products and waited to see whether the sales rolled in to determine success rates. Now, social media allows companies to have a dialogue with its customers and gain valuable feedback and input as it creates the message.

- **Become a consumer of content.** Content used to be something that very few people created. Reporters, TV anchors, movie directors, authors, radio DJs, and magazine editors created content, and everyone else consumed it. Now, everyone is a publisher, and the people who use the content are also the ones who create it. Content readers are not only consumers; they are also content publishers. Companies must consume the content of their target audience, in addition to publishing content.

The content pillar

- **Join the conversation.** Information and messaging for a company was once controlled by its marketing and sales departments. Now, with the democratization of information, no one owns the message about a product or company. Every company must become part of the conversation or risk letting users become the voice of the company.

- **Create engaging core content.** Social media is not just about content or messaging in a different format. The tools allow for creating interactive content that connects with consumers. Utilize this.

- **Manage the experience.** The money is in creating and managing the *experience*, not selling a product. The value of a book is not in its format; it's in the experience someone gets when reading it. The value is in how the author made the reader feel. Musicians can charge more money for a concert than a CD for the same reason: because the concert is not just a series of songs, but rather an experience where the musician connects with the audience.

- **Become a filter.** Television stations and newspapers are no longer king when it comes to filtering and sharing news. People are more likely to get their news by reading Trending Topics on Twitter, and they are more likely to share a link to a friend's blog post than MSN's homepage. By sharing content, you are actually creating it.

To build a platform, you must work consistently at both of these pillars. The Disney Channel adopted building a platform as a business model long before social media forced companies to consider it. So let's take a closer look at the social media success factors that enable your company to build a platform.

12 social media success factors

There are social media success factors that you control, and factors that are affected more by the community. This is one element of social pollination – you must have a fan base of existing heavy users on your channel to get any sort of traction on that channel.

The rest of your success depends heavily on community factors, which round out the last 5 factors in this list. You don't have as much control over these factors, but it's important to know about them. The more you optimize and grow your platform, the more likely you will be successful at social pollination.

Profile

Every social media site in the world has some sort of profile section. This is where you fill out information about yourself or your company. It is the base for all your contact information, interests, and social activity on the website.

Your profile is what attracts other users to connect (or not connect) with you on the social media site. If you have a great profile, it can help increase your connections on the network.

Here are some tips for optimizing any social media profile:

Use an image.

Upload a headshot or a logo to every social media profile you own. This image will represent you in every aspect of your social media activity. Keep your headshot consistent across social media sites so people recognize you easily if they want to connect on more than one.

Use your real name.

Hiding your true identity online is in the past. Sharing your real name is authentic, and helps your company build trust. It also holds you accountable for every piece of communication that goes out.

Even if you are managing a social media profile for your company, it's important to be transparent while still managing employee attrition. For example, on Twitter, the best set-up is to secure your company name as the handle, and list in the profile the names of the actual people who are tweeting.

Secure your usernames.

For example, Facebook allows you to shorten that ugly link to your profile or fan page. (Log in to Facebook and go to http://facebook.com/username to see if you are eligible.)

Do not get fancy with your username.

Instead, keep it professional and relevant to your business. Secure the same username for your company and key individuals in your company on every social media site for consistency. You can check NameChk (http://namechk.com) to check whether your username is available on over 130 different social media sites.

Provide every last bit of information.

Your goal is to have a content rich social media profile that lets others know what your company does. Keep the content interesting, fresh, unique, and clever to attract others to your profile. Demonstrate your company's expertise to gain credibility.

Also, make sure you add links to your other social media profiles. Most profiles have options to include a link to your blog and the popular media sites, like Twitter, Facebook, LinkedIn, Flickr, and YouTube. Use them.

Set your profile to public.

There are very few downsides to having a public profile, especially when you are using the account for business. You want search engines, current customers, and people who you have not yet met to be able to find you.

Use search engine friendly keywords in your profile.

What does your company want to be known for? Social media profiles are indexed by all the major search engines, and most social media sites also have their own search functions. Make sure your profile is filled with keywords that are important to your company and industry for search rankings.

Keep your goals in mind.

Do not use your company profile for pure socialization – use the profile to advance your business. Friendly-professional communication is okay, but controversial opinions or inappropriate language will turn customers off. Each time you post, think back to why you joined the site, and make sure you are furthering your company's goals, not just playing around with the tools.

Connections

Friends, fans, followers, subscribers – what's the difference? While there are nuances between these different titles, they are all really one thing: connections.

Friends are mutual connections where each party wants a relationship with the other. Often, users will only add friends whom they know in real life, or whom they converse with regularly online and have developed a friendship with.

Fans, followers, and subscribers are also similar in nature. "Fan" generally refers to people who follow companies or celebrities, while "follower" is often someone who follows an individual not of celebrity status. Fans are more likely to be people who simply admire the company and want to stay updated, while followers are looking for information from a specific source. Subscribers are often more involved. They want information, but more specifically, they don't want to miss any content you put out. This indicates a higher loyalty to your company.

Each social media site has its own lingo for the concept of connections, so don't get too hung up on any specific term. The important point is that the more genuine connections you have, the more successful you can be on social media, because sharing starts with you sharing within your network. Thus, the bigger your network is, the further your message can spread.

But be warned: building connections is **not** a numbers game. It's a **people** game. You have to like and care about people to create connections. There is no short cut. Building relationships is a huge part of social media, so don't try to circumvent the process.

Here are some tips for gaining more connections:

Use your current assets.

Even when you first join a social media site, you should not be starting from scratch. In fact, if you have aligned your social media channels to your company and goals, you probably already have a fan base on each social media site – you just haven't connected with them yet.

Most social media sites have tools to import connections from your email address book. Every business has a contact list of some sort.

Take your contact list (as a .csv file) and upload it to a Gmail account (you can create a special one for free just for this purpose) using the import features under contacts. Because most social media sites support importing contacts from Gmail, you can connect with current customers on any social media site.

Ask your network what they want.

Then give it to them. Answer questions, explain concepts, and share quotes and humor (related to your business).

Think of content your network does not want, but would like or need anyway. Engage people in your business with fun facts about your industry, news in your industry, or celebrities in your industry.

Signature

A signature is a short message that is appended to all your social activity on the site. Signatures are similar to profiles, but they are usually more limiting. The benefit of a signature is that you the more you use the site, the more often people will see whatever message you use.

Signatures are prominently used in email, blogs, and on forums. Very few social networks or bookmarking sites use signatures, but some do. You use a signature to tell people a little about yourself, and also tell people how to contact you.

Here are a few ways to optimize your signature:

Customize your signature with HTML.

Add your company logo or images that make your signature unique. You can also add color, change the font style, or increase/decrease the size. If you use Gmail, AOL, Yahoo, or Hotmail, you can customize your HTML with a Firefox extension called WiseStamp (http://wisestamp.com).

Rotate your signature.

If you email the same people several times, you can send them a different message each time to promote different articles, products, or social media accounts. The same is true for a blog; regular readers do not need to see the same message every time they visit.

Use only your most important links.

Choose one or two links to put in your signature, max. The fewer options you give the recipient, the higher your conversion rate will be.

Groups

Groups are prominent on most social media sites, but especially on social networking sites. Groups help organize people by their self-selected interests, making it easier for people to find and network with others like them.

Groups are used primarily to build community. Staying active in groups will help you build a network of like-minded people, who are more likely to take an interest in your products.

Here are a few ways to use groups to your advantage:

Find groups related to your products and get to know the administrator.

Administrators (Admins) are the gatekeepers of every group. They are able to delete comments, remove unruly members, and message the entire group with on click of the button. If you want to share a message with the entire group, it helps to know the gatekeepers.

Participate in groups.

Leave comments, start topics, ask questions, and create subgroups. The more you participate, the easier it will be for you to attract group members to your network.

Create groups that do not exist already.

Is there a group related to your product that has not been created? On Facebook, there is a fan page for "Hoodies." The group has 600,000 fans and is one of the most popular groups on the site. If you were a retail store, wouldn't you want to own this group?

Build membership in groups you administer.

People often only join one or two groups in their interest areas. Why should they join yours? The most valuable groups are the ones with the most people and the best content. Ask all of your established contacts to join your group so that others join as well. You can even ask your current group members to invite new ones.

Categories

While groups classify people by interest, categories classify content by interest. You can use categories to help others find your content. There is also a main page for most content-sharing sites that has links to all the hottest topics. For example, Digg has a main page for the most relevant links.

Category pages are also full of links to the hottest topics, but only those in the category. So it is easier to get to the front page for a category because there is less competition than the main page of the whole website. Category pages are also ranked in search engines for keywords, so it is valuable to be listed on a category page.

You can find category pages on blogs, bookmarking sites, and any other link or content-driven sites.

Here's how you can optimize your use of categories:

Add as many relevant categories as possible to your content.

The more categories you have attached to your content, the more people who are browsing each different category will see it.

Use categories for research.

Figure out what topics are popular, and which have been beaten into the ground. Write complimentary, original content, compared to what already exists. Content has a much better chance of going viral when it covers topics that no one else has covered, or takes a different angle than the way the topic has been covered before.

You can also quickly learn who your competitors for content are by looking at who is linked to on category pages of social media sites.

Use categories to find relevant information to share.

Because sharing on social media is in some ways, just as

important as creating on social media, categories can help your company find useful links quickly.

Feeds

Feeds allow you to organize and store information that you can share to social media sites automatically. You can create an RSS feed from any type of content, but the most common kind is a blog.

Social networking sites like Facebook and Amazon allow you to import your blog (or any other type of feed). Friendfeed is a service that lets you import feeds from all sorts of social networking sites like Flickr and YouTube, and keeps links to all your content in one place. Whenever you update the source of the feed, the content is also updated in every place you have imported your feed.

Here are some tips on using feeds for sharing:

Import everywhere.

Any time you can import, it's a good idea. Not only does it provide you with more views, but people share via social platforms. When you put your content on a social platform, it has more opportunity to be shared.

Feed more than just your blog posts.

You can create feeds for all sorts of content, including quotes and tips. I feed content from Google Reader to share on social media platforms like Twitter.

Manipulate your feeds.

You can use a service like Yahoo! Pipes to explore a variety of ways to manipulate your feeds. I have not dug into this much, but if you search for Yahoo! Pipes you will undoubtedly

Buzz Tip: Use Google Reader to share relevant links on Twitter or any other social media site

If you use Google Reader, the reader comes with a "blog" of items you've shared. To find your "blog," click on "Shared Items" in the left sidebar. A message in your main window says "Your shared items are available publicly at this web page." Click on the link to find the blog, and then click on "Atom Feed" on the right sidebar to get the feed for your "blog."

Now, use Twitterfeed (http://twitterfeed.com) to automatically post this feed to your Twitter account. I set mine up to check the feed every 30 minutes and to use the Title of the Post with a link.

I have over 200 feeds in my reader, and I can go through them in less than ten minutes per day. How? I scan the titles. In the right-hand corner, you have a choice to view your feeds in "Expanded" or "List" – use the "List" format to scan titles quickly for the most relevant headlines your Twitter audience would care about. When I find something I think might be good, I read it, then hit "Share" at the bottom of the post.

The post shows up in my Twitter stream within the hour. I've nearly doubled my number of followers by implementing this strategy, and I receive numerous retweets every day, which gives my brand more exposure and reach.

find some creative ideas for manipulating feeds to enable more sharing.

Contests and promotions

Contests and promotions give people a reason to take action. You can use them to let people know you exist, and to give current customers a reason to talk about your company or product with their friends.

Contests and promotions will create short-term results only if the incentives are aligned with the consumer's goals. Even then, companies cannot sustain the growth that happens during a promotion because once the incentive is gone, the interest goes with it.You can run a contest on any social media platform.

Here are several ways to optimize your contest:

Find a topic that people are passionate about.

Sports, pets, kids, and hobbies are fun topics to use in a contest. Avoid taboo topics that people may have strong opinions about, like religion or politics.

Leverage your current assets.

You will get much more out of a contest or promotion when you leverage what your company is already good at. If you are a consultant, don't give away a free iPod--give away an hour of your services. When you adjust your incentives to match the type of people you want to attract (ie: someone who wants an hour of your services) you can develop a much better lead list.

Make it easy for entrants to participate.

Video and essay contests are engaging, but may be too

difficult for many potential entrants. Keep it simple by asking entrants for five minutes or less of their time. You can ask for more, but you will get far fewer participants.

Hedge your contest prize.

Consider return on investment when running a contest or promotion. How much is one contest participant worth to you? One guy offered a chance to win an Adobe AIR to everyone who commented on a certain blog post. While he expected the contest to go viral, he ended up only receiving 8 comments. In contrast, another guy offered a laptop to one of his followers if he hit 500,000 on Twitter by a certain date. He didn't hit half a million (and didn't have to spring for the laptop prize), but he did gain thousands more followers just by running the promotion.

The main page

Several social media sites have a main page, or a summary area for all the activity and content that has taken place on the site. If your content is featured on this page, you get more traffic and visibility to your brand and your blog.

Social bookmarking sites, review sites, and even Twitter's trending topics section are all examples of a main page or area of popular content. In most cases, there is a ranking system that lets content move up and down on the page.

Create content like the content on the main page.

Use content that is already on the main page to understand what topics and what formats do the best.

Experiment with the algorithm, or talk to people who have.

It's really important to understand how to get to the main

page of the sites you are targeting. For example, on YouTube, if you can get about 100,000 views within 48 hours, your video will likely show up on the front page. To get into Twitter's Trending Topics, you need x number of tweets within a minute – depending on the time of day. You can get some of this information just by observing the timing of what's on the front page, or you can ask power users of the site for this information.

Power users

Every community has power users – the people who use the site the most. According to research done by Vassilis Kostakos, a professor at Carnegie Mellon University, a large portion of every website's content is created by a small portion of its users. For example, a small handful of Amazon users have rated hundreds of items on the site. But even the top 5% of active Amazon users on average rate less than ten items total. Similarly, Wikipedia gets millions of page views every month, but 1% of its users make half the edits to the site.

There are power users on every site, but power users dominate social bookmarking and review sites. Many voting algorithms weigh power users heavier than other users, so a vote from a power user can be worth much more. You will do better in social media if you can become friends with the most active users on the sites you are targeting. While you can't control what those people do, they are the influencers who can make things happen. Power users are, in some sense, similar to what traditional media was 5 years ago. Power users are the new gatekeepers.

Find the power users.

Of course, you could work to become one of the power users, but it is probably easier just to become friends with them.

Some sites will have a public rankings list, while others will just have an underground network of power users. Amazon, for example, has a rankings list of all their top reviewers, so it's easy to figure out who they are.

Network with purpose.

It's silly to target power users just because they are power users. You can build a better relationship when you have content that is of interest to the user. Look at the bookmarks and product reviews the person has already written and focus your efforts on the people who align best with you.

Pitch when you have a big push.

You do not need to submit every article or product to your power user friends. Instead, whenever you have a huge push, make sure you create content targeted at the power users you are friends with. Save your requests and favors for when you need something publicized.

Voting

Voting can be used to rank either content or users. For example, when you vote for a link on Digg, you are ranking the content. When you vote for a Yelp review as being helpful, you are voting for the person who wrote the review. You want to get more votes for both your profile and your content on every social media site you participate on.

Any social media site that has a main section to rank content or users uses some sort of voting. On Facebook, you click "like," on Twitter, you retweet, and on Amazon, you star good products. On YouTube, the vote that gets your content to the main page is total views.

Here's how to get more votes for both you and your content:

Go Viral: The Main Page, Power Users, Votes, and Timing

The way to get to the main page of any website is to get power users to vote for your content and encourage their friends to vote for your content. That's why you need to optimize your content and your network for all three of these social media success factors.

The final factor is timing. You can think of timing as both the time of day or week your content is submitted, and how many votes you get in a certain amount of time. Here are some ideas:

Digg – You need about 100 votes (diggs) in 30 minutes to hit the main page of Digg.

Twitter – Use Trendistic (http://trendistic.com) to find data for the day and time of day you are interested in. On a typical Monday at lunchtime, you need at least 5 tweets per minute consistently to become a trending topic.

YouTube – Get 100,000 views in 48 hours to hit the main page of YouTube.

Amazon – Sell 300 books a day to hit the Amazon bestseller list.

You can learn how to do this with **any** site that uses main pages, power users, and votes by observing the network's main page, learning what content works best, and building a platform on that network.

Use the tools.

If you are using the tools just to push your message, you lose. Make sure you are voting on other people's profiles and content – it makes them more likely to reciprocate when you put out something really good.

Create the best content.

If you have good content, people will rate both your content and your profile higher. Because people trust the wisdom of crowds, those ratings actually matter.

Ask your network.

If you've developed relationships, you can ask your friends to help you out with voting. You have to build the platform and the network first though, before you can successfully drive voting.

Comments and forums

Because they are so popular with the public, using social forums and commenting on content makes sense for anyone who wants to market their product on the internet. Jakob Nielsen, leading expert on usability design, did a study that found that only 1% of users contribute actively, 9% of users contribute regularly, and 90% of online community users are lurkers who read without contributing. That means that despite the size of a network, very few people will interact with all your content. The people who do are the ones you should focus on for promotions and help with voting.

Forums are the original social media. Just like you could start the conversation by starting a new thread in a forum, you can now start the conversation by posting new content to a social forum. Social forums are everywhere: blogs, social networks, and anywhere you can produce content.

Also, comment sections can play a huge part in your efforts to go viral on a social media site. The more conversation you have on your submission, the more votes you will get.

Here are ways some ways to get more comments on your content:

People participate in already active discussions.

You can NOT fake a conversation with multiple accounts, but you can ask close friends to comment on your content every once in awhile. It also helps to ask a question, ask for an opinion, or welcome people to share their opinions in the comments.

Respond to comments.

It not only increases the total number of comments you have (which encourages more people to participate), but it's also nice to build relationships with your most active participants.

Moderate comments on your content.

Having a comment policy and adding spam protection helps people feel comfortable leaving messages on your content.

Tagging

Folksonomy is a social classification method where the community works together to tag and categorize content. It's used mostly on social bookmarking sites and blogs, but you'll also find tagging features on sites like Flickr and YouTube. Tagging lets people organize content the way that makes sense to them, and also share that content with others.

Tags can also be viewed as pages, which rank in search engines. That means that showing up at the top of a page for a popular tag that ranks highly in search engines could bring lots of valuable traffic. With popular tagging sites, like Digg and Delicious, your tags can rank highly for keywords on search engines.

Tag items first with as many relevant tags as you can.

Although others can tag content however they want, you can help them by tagging it first. Many people will choose their tags based on the tags that are suggested to them already. The more tags you use, the more likely your content is to get found on a social network site.

Use keyword research to improve tagging.

If you tag your content with unique keywords, you can use social media to rank in search engines. In upcoming chapters, you will learn more about keyword research.

Summary

Building a platform is the first step to success on social media. To build a platform, you must first build two pillars:

- Relationship Pillar

- Content Pillar

You can build a better platform and encourage sharing by leveraging the following 7 social media success factors:

- Profile

- Connections

- Signature

- Groups

- Categories

- Feeds

- Contests and promotions

You also learned five more community-driven social media success factors:

- The main page

- Power users

- Voting

- Comments

- Tagging

The Psychology of Online Sharing

CareerBuilder launched a publicity campaign called Age-o-Matic in 2007. Age-o-Matic was designed specifically to go viral with no marketing spend; the goal was to put CareerBuilder at the center of the job dissatisfaction discussion by poking fun at how job dissatisfaction causes people to age prematurely.

Users uploaded an image of them and answered a short survey about how bad their current job was. They could then animate the image say whatever they wanted, and could email the animated image to their friends.

The results were phenomenal:

- 2 million unique visitors to the site

- 50 million media impressions across major television, print and online outlets in the first month

- 40 news broadcasts, including national programs like CNN and E!

- Articles in national publications, including USA Today (twice), AdWeek, and Advertising Age

What made the campaign so successful? The campaign was successful thanks to a combination of several psychological factors, which you will learn in this chapter.

But perhaps the greatest lesson you can learn from CareerBuilder is to create your content with sharing in mind from the beginning. If you have content and you are trying to figure out how to make it go viral, you've already lost.

So why do people share? Better yet, why don't people share? There are common reasons why people do or do not share online, and understanding them will give you insight into problems your company might face when launching a viral campaign.

10 ways to encourage people to share your online content

A person will share when:

- The tools are simple and intuitive

- The information is relevant to his peers

- The information fits within a framework, opinion, or belief the person already holds

- The information is cutting edge and has not been shared with her network already

- The information has also been shared by others

- The information is given with no strings attached

- The information is important enough to share

- The person has a reason to share

- The person can add her personal touch

- The person wants to see his friends succeed (and his enemies fail)

The tools are simple and intuitive

With new technology tools cropping up every day, visitors have limited time to figure out how your system works. If you want people to share your content, you must use tools that are simple and intuitive and integrate well into your message.

Simple reminders like a link in an email broadcast to "Share with a friend," or sharing tools that allow people to share on the network(s) of their choosing, always help.

Simple and intuitive tools are a small reason for why people share, but if your company overlooks this detail, even the best content will not be shared. Luckily, most social networks already incorporate intuitive sharing into the platform. If your platform is lacking in tools, use the ShareThis or AddThis button to give your consumers an easy way to share.

The information is relevant to his peers

In organizations, information travels peer-to-peer, but does not transcend to higher (or lower) levels. There are many reasons for this (trust, office politics, time constraints) but remember that organizations mirror society in this respect.

The only way to reach your audience is almost always to *reach their peers* and convince them the information is relevant.

This means that reaching the topmost influencers (like celebrities, athletes, or major television networks) is not as necessary as some may lead you to believe. Not only is it difficult to reach these influencers, but it is easier to reach them by reaching the people influenced by them first. Influencers have no choice but to pay attention to the crowd; so reach enough of the crowd, and you will reach the influencers eventually.

The information fits within a framework, opinion, or belief the person already holds

While some would say controversy is a good way to gain publicity, the way to generate sharing is when you say something new about a popular opinion that is already widely understood.

This is not to say controversy doesn't work. Controversy works when there are many people who hold one of two opposing opinions; for example, in politics when you are either for or against a policy. In these cases, though, the person will share the content that represents her opinion only. Controversy works simply because the issue is polarizing and creates teamwork on each side, sending both sides of the argument viral.

The information is cutting edge and has not been shared with her network already

There is something about being the first person to do

something or being in the know when no one else is that appeals to many people. People will share when the information is new, unique, and has not been shared heavily within the person's network already. Once the information has been shared heavily, the desire to share it is decreased.

The information has also been shared by others

While most people would love to be the original discoverer of new information, social proof is still huge on social media and any online content. This seems to conflict with the rule about sharing what has not been shared before, so let me explain.

Social proof is all about other strangers sharing the information; someone may still feel compelled to share if the information has not been shared with *her* network yet. The best time to reach someone with your message is when you have social proof that the message is shared, and when they are the first *in their group of friends* to learn about the message.

The information is given with no strings attached

People like to try before they buy. Whenever you ask them to subscribe or sign-up for your service without demonstrating the value, they are quick to leave the page. But it is not enough to *say* your content is valuable. You have to show the person the content and let them decide whether it is valuable or not.

At the same time, it is important to collect information in order to measure results, which is why so many companies require sign-ups or subscriptions in the first place.

The key is *balance*. There are several techniques you can use to balance free (no strings attached) content and paid (sign-up, subscription, or cost) content.

- Provide introductory material for free, but charge for advanced materials. This will get people in the door, but it will not impress people who are looking for the advanced techniques only.

- Provide material for free, and support, customization, or individual consulting for a fee

- Provide 90% of material for free and charge for the big secret, the one that ties everything together

The information is important enough to share

There is a chain letter that has been circulating since the early days of the internet claiming that women who wear ponytails while running are at a higher risk of getting raped. The claim is completely false, yet people continue to share it.

But rape is a serious crime that stimulates fear in women and the men who love them. People want to share this preventative information with their daughters, sisters, and wives.

When you create a message that fuels strong emotion and carries a sense of importance, people will be more likely to share it.

The person has a reason to share

A product may be high-quality and still have no one talking about it. Why? Because just having good products is never enough; you have to give people a reason to share!

One easy way to give someone a reason to share your message is by coining a term or being the very best in your industry. Become synonymous with a word or a concept, and people will continue to think and talk about you whenever they hear it. For example, you can't hear the word "twilight" without thinking of vampires. Your product needs a signature.

According to Mark Hughes, author of *Buzzmarketing*, there are six buttons of buzz: the taboo, the unusual, the outrageous, the hilarious, the remarkable, or the secrets. Do you give people a reason to buzz about you?

The person can add her personal touch

People prefer to reinvent something, adding their personal touch before passing it on. Flickr is a site for sharing photos, but one of the largest sections of the site is called the Creative Commons area. This is a place where you can find interesting images and use them in various ways – in a blog post, on Facebook, and so forth. You can add captions, remix the image, create a photo montage, write content, or add music. You can even print the images on any object you want.

Many people feel their jobs are mundane or uncreative, so people love any chance they have to do something creative. Give people a way to personalize and re-share, and they will happily pass along your message.

The person wants to see his friends succeed (and his enemies fail)

It's true. The more true friends (not just Twitter or Facebook friends) you have, the more your good content will be shared.

Let's go back to Age-o-Matic. The campaign used almost all of these factors to induce sharing. The tools were simple and intuitive and there were no strings attached to trying the tools. The idea fit within a framework – that of disliking your current job – and it created an enemy out of your company and a friend out of CareerBuilder, which would help you get out of your situation. The message was customizable, so people could personalize it, and the personalization and humor gave people a reason to share. Furthermore, the content was relevant to peers, and no one else – you would never share the email with a boss or people who worked under you – only people on the same level in the same situation. Finally, the sharing took place over email – which meant that unless you had received the email from someone else, you knew the content would be fresh when you sent it out.

All companies dream of creating a viral campaign like Age-o-Matic, but there are several things that can stand in your way, even if you master these 10 sharing reasons. Let's talk about reasons your content will not be shared.

10 reasons people won't share your online content

Understanding why someone would not share your content is just as important as understanding why someone would. Make any combination of these 10 mistakes and you will have difficultly spreading information and content online.

A person will not share because:

- The copy does not appeal to him

- The content is not delivered in the right format

- The content is boring/mediocre/stagnant

- The person does not understand the content or the technology to share it

- The person does not have the opportunity to share

- The person is competitive, or he is not a natural team player

- The person's online friends do not share her interests

- The person does not want to be misunderstood

- The person is embarrassed or has chosen not to reveal her true identity

- The person feels manipulated

The copy does not appeal to him

Jeff Sexton, a guest writer for the popular blog Copyblogger, writes about four different types of headlines that appeal to different types of people: the spontaneous, methodical, competitive, and humanistic.

Most copy only appeals to one of these four types of people, which limits the reach of the message. If you can create messages that appeal to more than one personality type, your message will be shared. We will talk about headlines and titles in much greater depth in the chapter about copywriting and SEO.

The content is not delivered in the right format

People learn in different ways: some visually, some aurally, some by doing, and others by skimming text. People also prefer longer text and content over shorter content. Online, it is helpful to test several different types of content to see how consumers respond.

Content formats that people love to share include:

- Resource lists

- Emotional stories or examples

- Mind maps and bird's-eye views

- Interactive or dynamic content

- Visually stimulating content, like videos

Not all of these types of content will be a great match for your company, or a great match for your reader, which is why it is important to experiment.

The person does not understand the content or the technology to share it

People are reluctant to admit that they don't understand something. They would rather ignore the information and forget about it. One thing for sure is that no one will share content that doesn't make sense to them.

Technology is constantly changing, and even the simplest tasks that we understand become a barrier to others' sharing. This is a good time to talk about channels, because most people have preferences for what channels they prefer to use for communication. Some people would rather filter requests and communication through their email inbox, while others want to be able to pick up the phone and get answers right away.

Depending on the demographics of your consumer base, you may have to educate them on how to share content via email or social media outlets.

The content is boring/mediocre/ stagnant

We all know content needs to be interesting, cutting edge, and fresh. People want entertainment. According to the Ruder Finn Intent Index, at least 92% of people go online to learn, have fun, and socialize. With so many websites to turn to, why should someone choose yours?

People only share a small amount of what they learn. In an attention-seeking economy, no one wants to recommend what they consider to be "the obvious" to their friends. People always want the newest and most innovative content, and they will only share the cream of the crop when it comes to content.

As the digital world gains more and more content, the standards for fresh content are rising, and the bar is set higher all the time.

The person does not have the opportunity to share

Some products lend themselves to natural conversation and sharing. For example, it's easy to tell you how comfortable my 6 inch heels are when you see me walking a mile in them because you will notice something unusual and comment on it. Other products are not easy to discuss in every day conversation; for example, I rarely discuss how comfortable my couch is unless someone visits my home.

Online sharing works the same way and products that would come up in natural conversations are also more likely to come up naturally in online interactions. Consider how your product can enter natural conversations, and it will also be-come easier to share online.

The person is competitive, or he is not a natural team player

People want exclusivity because it's good to be in the know; to have the secrets that no one else has, especially when those secrets give that person an advantage in business.

Likewise, some people work better individually, and prefer to look up information when it's needed, and on their own. People who are self-sustaining assume others are self-sus-taining too, so they are less likely to share information that wasn't requested.

In both these cases, extremely valuable information, partic-ularly for business, will not be shared readily because it was not requested.

The person's online friends do not share her interests

This can be network specific. For example, I love guilty plea-sure teen drama shows, but I never talk about that on my Twitter feed, where I mostly connect with business profes-sionals. Vice-versa, I never share links about social media tactics for business with my Facebook friends from high school and college.

People want to share content on a network only if it is rel-evant to their network, which is why you must give them several social network options for sharing.

The person does not want to be misunderstood

Because 70% of our communication is in non-verbal cues, it is very easy for people to get confused with online communications. Sometimes promoting a radical new idea or sharing someone else's opinion can be daunting when the person has not sorted out which side of the fence she is on.

The person is embarrassed or has chosen not to reveal her true identity

There are topics people don't want to share with others because it's not natural. Information about sex, health problems, personal issues, or relationships could all be considered taboo among networks of people. This is especially true on social networks because of the public nature of the information and the lasting, searchable record each blog post or Tweet creates.

Some people also prefer to remain anonymous online, or are forced to remain anonymous online because of work. Sharing too much gives the person's identity away.

Finally, some people like having alter-personas. They want to keep their friends separate from their coworkers because they get to reinvent their personality with each group.

The person feels manipulated

When you watch a show like Penn & Teller, do you spend most of your time trying to figure out, "How did they do that?!"

When asked how Penn & Teller's show became so popular, Teller explains, "The magic show is a competition. The audience is trying to figure you out. They aren't suspending their disbelief—they're trying to expose you as a scam artist."

As humans, we dislike things we do not understand and we hate when we are tricked. Just as a viewer is suspicious of magic tricks, consumers are suspicious of brands that market themselves online. There are legions of spammers who use unethical techniques to trick web surfers into giving up personal information or clicking on harmful links. These are all negative expectations that your company must overcome to gain trust from consumers.

The bottom line on sharing

The bottom line when it comes to sharing is that people make judgments about content based on how they feel when they consume it. That means when people have a horrible day, they are less likely to share. When they are having a great day they will share with the world.

You cannot control the day-to-day emotions of your followers, but you can control some aspects of the experience a user has when they consume your content.

- Do they gain insight? They will be more likely to share.

- Do you give them a resource that they want to come back to? They will be more likely to share.

- Did they get bored at the halfway point? You will probably lose them before they even consider sharing.

If you are going to rely on social pollination for your business, you must understand the psychology of what gets people to share, and what keeps them from sharing. Use this guide as a checklist for every piece of viral content you create. Use the guide at the early stages of content creation, when you are coming up with a concept, and before you've done all the heavy duty work to turn that concept into reality. You will not have much success creating viral content without keeping these tips in mind.

Change the experience of talking about you so people will choose to do it.

Five minutes of action – Schedule a mini content review workshop

Choose a marketing communication your company actually uses to promote its products or services. It can be the main page of your site, a blog post, or a direct mailing piece.

Send this checklist to the people attending the meeting. Ask the meeting attendees to complete an evaluation exercise. Have each attendee go through these checklists and make notes of what the communication does well, and what it does not.

At the meeting, give everyone a chance to share his or her critique. Take notes and assign action items to get the marketing piece ready for sharing online!

Summary

In this chapter, we talked about why people share content online, and why they don't. Before your company creates any viral content, review these guidelines and make sure you've given your content the best potential for online sharing. I also strongly recommend the mini content review workshop, because it's easier to recognize potentially viral content when you've experienced creating it firsthand!

Learn More

Dan Zarella (http://danzarella.com) – Dan Zarella is a viral marketing scientist who specializes in social media. He does research to understand how messages are shared on the web.

Content Ideas

Social media is about developing relationships with your customers and providing value in the form of products, services, and ideas. But at some point, you will have to provide content for the social media channels you decide to use in order to gain attention from the audience you are targeting. This takes time that, as a small company, you may not feel you have.

To build an online presence, however, you don't necessarily have to create every piece of content yourself. There are plenty of places you can get free content to use.

You could also become a filter for information and tips in your industry. Because of the massive amount of information online, combined with shortened attention spans of web surfers, there is a large need for content filtering. By filtering others' content and adding your own ideas, you can still build relationships and establish yourself or your company as an expert in your industry.

The good news is you can find and create content quickly, even without a budget to hire a writer to do it for you. You have choices when providing content: you can get the content from someone else or create it yourself.

5 ways to let others create content for you (from easiest to hardest)

If you are struggling to create content, there are several ways you can circumvent the process of writing content from scratch.

Public domain content

Public domain is any content that is not copyrighted or owned by anyone. That means there are no legal restrictions on use and you can legally publish or reprint these works for any purpose, including commercial purposes; but I would recommend you remix these works and edit them to suit your purposes instead.

Public domain is not limited to written content; you can also find music or images to use and remix as you like in videos, podcasts, and print.

You can find public domain content from the following resources:

Public domain books and text

- Project Gutenberg (http://www.gutenberg.org/)

- Authorama (http://www.authorama.com/)

- Internet Public Library (http://www.ipl.org/div/subject/browse/hum60.60.00/)

- WikiNews Articles (http://en.wikinews.org/wiki/Category:Public_domain_articles)

Public domain music

- PD Info (http://www.pdinfo.com/)

- Choral Public Domain Library (Sheet music) (http://www.cpdl.org/wiki/index.php/Main_Page)

- Open Source Music (http://www.opensourcemusic.com/)

- PD Music (http://www.pdmusic.org/)

Public domain images

- Flickr Creative Commons (http://flickr.com/creativecommons)

- Public Domain Pictures (http://www.publicdomainpictures.net/)

- Public Domain Photos (http://www.public-domain-photos.com/)

- Public Domain Images (http://www.public-domain-image.com/)

It might take some time to sort through these resources to find the content you need, but it could be worth the time especially if you are on a budget. Remember, before you use any of that content, check the usage rights and keep a record of how you have used the content.

Buzz Tip: Private Label Rights

Private label content is content that you purchase for a low price and can then edit and use for commercial purposes. It is similar to public domain content, but you pay a nominal fee to use it.

It is difficult to find private label content, but you can check out the PLR Store (http://ww.theplrstore.com/) to see if any topics are relevant to your industry or products.

Article banks

Article banks are websites where people who want to establish themselves as experts in their fields can write on the subject of their expertise. If you are looking for content for your newsletter, you can check the terms of use on these sites to see whether they allow republishing articles in exchange for an author attribution. Each site has its own terms and conditions, so read them carefully before using any of the content on the sites. Some sites may also require additional permission from the authors to use or edit the articles.

There are tons of article banks available for you to both publish articles and pull articles. Here are several you will want to check out:

- Amazines (http://www.amazines.com)

- Article Alley (http://www.articlealley.com)

- Articles Base (http://www.ArticlesBase.com)

- Article City (http://www.articlecity.com)

- Article Dashboard (http://www.articledashboard.com)

- Article Depot (http://www.articledepot.co.uk)

- Article Finders (http://www.articlefinders.com)

- Article Snatch (http://www.articlesnatch.com)

- Ezine Articles (http://www.ezinearticles.com)

- Go Articles (http://www.goarticles.com)

- Idea Marketers (http://www.ideamarketers.com)

- Isnare (http://www.isnare.com)

- Search Warp (http://www.searchwarp.com)

- Top 7 Business (http://top7business.com/)

Whether you pull articles from an article bank or not, you can also use the sites to find expert writers in your industry and contact them personally for permission to republish their content in your newsletter. Because it benefits both them and you, it should be fairly easy to get permission to use their content.

Guest writers

Another easy way to get content for your blog or newsletter is to recruit guest writers to write content. This is similar to finding articles in article banks, but you must find and manage the writers yourself.

There are several benefits to this method. You can handpick your experts, and you have more control over the content and quality. You can also ask for unique content that hasn't been posted in several article banks already, which will be better for search engine optimization. This method has downsides though. You must work harder to find writers, and you may need to pay for their services. You are also responsible for brainstorming topics and editing the content.

You can find guest writers by asking your network on your website, or through your social media accounts. Many bloggers are happy to contribute to other blogs, websites, and newsletters in exchange for author attribution links at the end of the article.

If your company has several employees, you can also create a group blog that several employees contribute to.

Interviews

If you are looking to build credibility, credibility by association is a wonderful way to create content. Often, others can provide more expertise or bring a new perspective to your topic. Find credible, interesting sources and contact them to set up an interview call. You can record the phone call and package it as a podcast on your site.

If you would prefer an even more hands-off method, you can also come up with questions and email them to your interviewee. Your interviewee will complete 80% of the work by answering the questions, and then you can simply edit and post on your site.

You can also use interviews to attract your target audience. CaptainU, a company that builds software to help high school athletes find placement on college teams, uses interviews from well-known athletes to build buzz about their website. This is good for inbound links and search engine optimization, in addition to being viral content just by nature.

The company also interviews college students who have used their software to make the team, and uses those interviews as testimonials for their software.

Interviews are a cool way to engage your audience on social

media and create viral content with limited effort on your part.

Resource lists

Because the internet needs organization, resource lists are highly viral by nature and always generate inbound links and sharing on social media sites.

To create a resource list, first find a topic that relates to your industry or product and do a quick search engine sweep to make sure the topic has not already been covered. Then use search engines to find useful links that should be included in your resource list.

Another way to find offbeat links is by checking out social bookmarking sites like Delicious. Delicious is built on a tagging system, so you can use the search feature to find articles that other users have tagged with your topic. The search feature also suggests related topics and tags, so you can find more unique content.

Once you have a list of resourceful links, put it together in a pretty package. Write a short summary of each link and explain why it's on the list, and add public domain pictures throughout your post to make the post visually interesting. Include the number of resources in your title and you have created a potentially viral piece of content for your blog or website.

More Long Content Ideas

If you are writing a blog, you should always have pillar content – content that is detailed, useful, and never goes out of date. Pillar content is about 1000-3000 words (about the length of a magazine article), and the idea is to attract links and readership to your blog. Spend an hour or two writing pillar content once every 2 weeks.

To fill in the gaps between pillar content, here are some more blog post ideas:

- **News posts** – Write a short opinion piece about news in your industry, with a link to the original source.

- **Reviews** – Write a book or product review about something related to your field. If you are one of the first reviewers, your blog can attract a great deal of traffic from search engines.

- **Profiles** – Instead of reviewing a product, why not review a person in your industry? You can talk about the person's history and contributions to your industry.

- **Case Studies** – Many people learn best through example, so sharing case studies from your industry (especially if they are new) establishes you as a thought leader.

- **Q&A** – Answer questions that come in through email on your blog. That way you can keep reusing the material you write every time you receive an email.

Short content that works everywhere

There is no reason to spend a ton of time creating content. When it comes to building a following, relationships count also. That's why short content is a trend in social media.

Most celebrities did not start connecting with their audience online until they learned about a new microblogging service called Twitter. Celebrities who never had time to blog were now using social media and 140 characters to talk to their fans.

Companies with limited time now have the means to connect with their customers without creating a ton of content. While blogs, newsletters, and articles are still the best ways to attract customers to your website, building relationships and interaction is much easier with short content on social media.

Another thing to remember about delivering content in the right format is behavioral science, particularly the theories about gains and losses. According to an article in the Harvard Business Review, people would rather win $5 twice than $10 once, despite the economic equality of these two outcomes. If you consider behavior science as it applies to social media, people would rather receive 5 pieces of short, salient tips than one long list.

Polls, surveys, questions, pictures, short video, salient tips, and quotes are all easy ways to create short content, so don't forget to mix in short content with longer content.

Repurposing your current content for different mediums

Your company has created promotional materials time and time again. If you are looking for new content, why not take your old content and repurpose it?

Use your blog posts, excerpts from a book, or past newsletters as articles and send them to trade journals, newspapers, and magazines for syndication. Offer to syndicate these articles for free if the publisher lists your website in return.

Circulate your articles online by feeding them to all your social networking profiles. Include links within the post back to your blog, your other social media profiles, or your products or services.

Turn your articles into podcasts by using the same information and creating a video or audio recording. Likewise, turn your videos and podcasts into articles by creating a transcript. Blinkx, Podzinger, and Podscope are three services that create transcripts from video and audio files.

Convert a post with five tips into 5 tweets or status updates on your favorite social network. Direct people back to the original article with a link in each update.

Pair each of your tips with a striking public domain image and republish it on popular photo-sharing sites. Then, print a coffee table book and use it as a promotional tool, give it as a gift to your most loyal customers, or sell it as a souvenir from your website or in your store.

Turn your 5 tips into a slideshow and upload it to a popular business website, like LinkedIn, Slideshare, Hubpages, or Squidoo. Host a webinar or schedule a lecture to generate leads and utilize these slides during the presentation. Then upload a recording of your audio plus the slides to your website or a video-sharing site so people who missed the presentation can view it on their own time.

Collect several of your articles, podcasts, or videos and package them as a more comprehensive book or CD. Create a membership site that allows members special access to premium content for a fee. Or give your most loyal customers free access as a bonus for purchasing a product or service.

Remember, people learn differently, and people absorb ideas better when they are in various formats. Using the same ideas, you can create new content in different mediums and reach a larger target audience than before.

Summary

The five ways to let others create content for you are:

- Remix public domain content

- Use articles banks for your newsletter

- Host guest writers

- Conduct interviews

- Create list posts

You should also incorporate pillar content to your blog and create a mixture of longer and shorter posts on each of your social website profiles. Finally, repurpose content you have already created to different mediums and different social websites to attract new audiences.

Optimize Your Content: Add Internet Copywriting and Search Optimization

You have created a viral message, but you still are not done! If you want people to share your content, you must also tend to two more details:

- People must be able to find your content

- The content must have appealing copy

In this chapter, you will learn enough about search optimization and internet copywriting to boost the sharing of your content.

Search Engine Optimization 101

Search engine optimization, or SEO, is an important aspect

of creating any content for social media. The idea is to take content that is written for people and optimize the content so it can be found by search engines.

You need to understand the two ways to optimize: on-page SEO and off-page SEO.

On-page SEO

On-page SEO relates mainly to adding relevant keywords to your site in various places to alert search engines to what your content is about.

The debate about whether on-page SEO actually matters is ongoing. Because of spammers and cheaters, search engines now place little emphasis on on-page SEO, relying more on off-page SEO since it is harder to manipulate. Still, it is valuable to do some on-page SEO because it's an aspect of SEO that you can control and most on-page SEO still counts for something. You can improve your on page SEO by:

Including keyword phrases in your meta tags (title, description, keywords for each page).

In your header section (before the </head> code) add the following tags:

<title>Your page title</title>

<meta name="description" content="fill in the description">

<meta name="keywords" content="fill in the keywords, separated by commas">

Use plug-ins.

If you are running a self-hosted Wordpress blog, you can use the Platinum SEO Pack plug-in to add the title, description, and keywords within your blog post editor.

Including keyword phrases in your URL address.

SEOMoz has put together a cheat sheet to explain the anatomy of a URL.

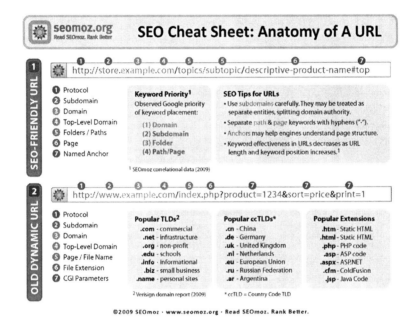

Include keyword phrases in your header tags.

The text within your H1, H2, and H3 tags is valuable – use it!

Include keywords in the alt and title tags for every image or graphic on your website.

You can do this by adding keywords and alternate text to this link code: <img src="website.com/source.jpg" alt="" title="" />

Once you have this done, construct and submit your site map to search engines so your website can be indexed. The construction is done for you if you have an RSS feed, and you create a sitemap using the sitemap generator at http://

www.Google.com/webmasters/sitemaps.

Use the sitemap to submit your website to search engines so they can crawl your pages. The more search engines you submit your sitemap to, the better; but if you are pressed for time, at least submit your sitemap to Google, Yahoo, MSN, Ask, and Bing.

Go to http://www.sitemapwriter.com/notify.php to submit your sitemap to these services.

Off-page SEO

Off-page SEO is what happens in other parts of the web, or off your webpage. There are many ways to improve your off-page SEO, but the main factors are:

The number and quality of inbound links to your site According to an article in New York Magazine, inbound links are an 80% accurate predictor of traffic to your site. If you want to rank in the search engines for your primary keyword phrases, focus on getting inbound links to various pages of your website.

Get inbound links by networking with blogs in your niche and providing valuable content those groups can link to.

Search for blogs about your topic on these sites:

- Technorati – http://technorati.com

- Alltop – http://alltop.com

Submit your best articles to blog carnivals.

Blog carnivals are lists of related links that a blogger (the blog carnival host) posts to his or her blog. Go to Blog Carnival (http://blogcarnival.com) to browse subject listings.

Use social bookmarking.

Many bloggers share links to their favorite articles on a blog or miniblog. When you use social bookmarking, you have a better chance of getting on someone's radar.

Comment on other blogs.

Most comment systems use a "rel=nofollow" tag which tells search engines not to count the link in determining page rank; however, a link is a link, and the more you have, the more traffic you can build for your site. Tip: Instead of linking to your main domain name, link to an article on your site that is about the same subject you are commenting on.

Publish articles in article banks.

We talked about article banks in the last chapter. While you can find great content for your newsletter on an article bank, you can also be the content provider, linking to your own (relevant) articles to create inbound links.

Use anchor text with inbound links.

Anchor text is the text that other sites use to link to your pages, rather than the URL address. You can boost the number of keywords you rank for by getting others to use your keywords as anchor text rather than yourdomainname.com. If you can get several sites to link to your page using the same anchor text phrase, you can rank highly for that keyword phrase in search engines. However, if you can get a mix of anchor text for the same page, you will rank for more keyword phrases overall.

When it comes to SEO, search engines rank individual pages of your website. You can have an subpage with a higher page rank than your main index page, so every page of your website can be optimized, whether it is the landing page or not. Many people will enter your domain through subpages that are more relevant to their search query than your main index page is.

While SEO is important, don't drive yourself nuts trying to stuff your website with keywords. Write for people, not search engines, and you will do much better in SEO since it is heavily based on inbound links from other sites (and other people). To optimize each of your pages, focus on offering high quality, relevant content that is heavily targeted for the people who are reading it. Give your visitors substantial information about your products and services in each and every article on your website. Then go back and optimize the page for your target keyword phrases so others will find you easily.

Keyword research

Generally a person's searches from a search engine like Google or Yahoo start with a general phrase, like "dog toys," and get narrowed down as the person gains a clearer understanding of what they are looking for.

After a few searches, a person might get more specific because the first search results page did not provide them with relevant results for what they were looking for. They might, for example, begin a new search with the phrase, "buy dog toys safe for Chihuahuas in Kansas." This phrase is not only more specific, but there are fewer searches for this phrase than "dog toys."

Long tail keyword theory suggests that you optimize your website for long keyword phrases that are more specific and more relevant for searching. Though they account for fewer searches than short keyword phrases, it is easier to rank high for them in search engine results.

Studies show that most people don't look past the first 3-5 results of their query, and less than 30% of web searches make it to the second page. The best keyword research strategy is to find long tail keywords with which you have a chance of appearing in the top few results on the first page of Google, Yahoo or MSN.

Free keyword research tools

If you are running a small business, you don't have time for endless hours of search engine optimization. When you are doing keyword research, use this quick, three step process to get your website to the 85% mark. I guarantee you will outrank most of your competitors.

Step 1 – Create a keyword phrase list based on your finished article. Do this just from reading the content and choose keywords that accurately reflect what your article is about.

Step 2 – Use free keyword tools to find keyword phrases that you haven't thought of and get estimates of traffic for your keyword phrases. When estimating traffic, it is less important to get accurate estimates and more important to compare the estimates between different keyword phrases so you know which to use.

Free tools to brainstorm new keywords:

- Spacky.com – http://spacky.com

- Keyword Spy - http://www.keywordspy.com/

- SpyFu – http://spyfu.com

- Quintura – http://quintura.com

- Wordtracker – http://freekeywords.wordtracker.com/

- NicheBotClassic – http://nichebotclassic.com/

- Google Suggest - http://tools.seobook.com/general/ keyword-information/

Free tools to estimate traffic:

- Google Traffic Estimator - https://adwords.google.com/select/TrafficEstimatorSandbox

- Adwords Keyword Tool - https://adwords.google.com/select/KeywordToolExternal

Free tools to make traffic comparisons between keywords:

- Google Trends – http://google.com/trends

- Google Insights – http://www.google.com/insights/search/

Step 3 - Check which keyword phrases you could rank higher for. Go to the largest search engine (currently Google) and search for your keyword phrase in quotation marks. Click on the first result, and get a Google page rank. If the page rank is 4 or less, you can probably rank for this keyword phrase fairly easily. You can also look at the number of ads for each phrase: the more ads, the more valuable the keyword is, and the harder it would be to rank for it.

When you use these three steps, remember you are searching for the long tail. You may start by looking at the keyword "librarians." When you see results, you notice "librarian jobs" is a popular term. Don't stop there; start your research over with the phrase "librarian jobs." Continue this cycle until you've drilled down to the long tail searches – these are the searches you have the best chance of ranking well for.

Search is going social

Most SEO is off-page at the moment. This could change as technology changes, but for now, social media is the hottest thing in search.

Dana Todd of Newsforce Search Engine Marketing Professional Organization (SEMPO) says that "Social media accounts for up to half the Top 10 search results for any given query." According to EMarketer.com, "Data from com-Score, GroupM and M80 indicates searchers are also more likely to keep a brand in mind if they have seen a combination of paid search ads and social media." The idea is that content's time of creation could be the most relevant factor in search results, and the best way to get the most up-to-date information is to search what people are saying and linking to on social media.

US Internet Users Who Search on Brand Product Terms, by Ad Exposure, 2009 (% of total)

Paid search only

23%

Relevant social media and paid search

38%

Influenced social media and paid search

65%

Note: read chart as saying that 23% of Internet users exposed to paid search ad then search on brand product terms
Source: comScore, GroupM Search and M80, "The Influenced: Social Media, Search and the Interplay of Consideration and Consumption," October 6, 2009

107406   www.**eMarketer**.com

Large search engine sites have placed their search algorithm in the hands of people ever since they made inbound links (essentially, "votes" from other websites) a high determining factor of page rank. Search has always been fairly democratic, but now, search engine giants like Yahoo and Google are seeing major search engine competition from social media sites like Facebook and Twitter. While each of these sites started as social media (a social network and a microblogging platform, respectively), they have both turned their

Buzz Tip: 4 search engines you have probably never heard of

Move over Google – the future of searching is no longer just about you! Check out these 4 new search engines below, then consider how to manage your company's brand on them.

OneRiot

OneRiot looks at what's happening on Twitter and Digg in real-time results. They write, "Increasingly, the web's most interesting content is what our friends and other people are talking about, sharing and looking at right now. However, when people search for that content, traditional search engines struggle to surface these fresh, socially-relevant results. That's the hole – and it's a big one – that OneRiot is filling."

http://oneriot.com

Wolfram

Wolfram's Alpha version allows users to compute their search engine results, rather than find links that will give them the information. In seconds, you can use Wolfram to find the phase of the moon from the day you were born. They write, "Wolfram|Alpha's long-term goal is to make all systematic knowledge immediately computable and accessible to everyone. We aim to collect and curate all objective data; implement every known model, method, and algorithm; and make it possible to compute whatever can be computed about anything."

http://wolfram.com/

Book of Odds

Book of Odds is a search engine 3 years in the making that helps people learn more about the odds of every day life. The authors write, "It is a destination where people come to learn about the things that worry or excite them, to read engaging and thoughtful articles, and to participate in a community of users that share their interests and ambitions. It contains hundreds of thousands of Odds Statements, from the odds of being the only one to survive a plane crash, to the odds of having a heart attack, to the odds of having ever eaten cold pizza for breakfast."

http://bookofodds.com/

Twine

Twine is, amazingly, completely unrelated to Twitter. But it capitalizes on the foundations of social media in that you can join groups based on what you're searching for, and "connect" with people who are searching for the same things. It actually looks like the search engine version of StumbleUpon. They write, "The more you use Twine, the smarter it gets. Fill out your profile to discover new info and interests through Twine's personalized recommendations." At the least, fill out your profile to reserve your name!

http://twine.com

Currently, none of these four search engines have much to say when I search for most small brands But take a look into your crystal ball – how will these engines change the way we manage brands in the future?

efforts to search as of late. Even though YouTube, the second largest search engine in the world, is owned by Google, it also represents the ever-growing presence of social media in search.

Social bookmarking sites are another way of finding answers, as sites like Digg and Delicious have implemented categories and tagging to organize the links found through their sites. OneRiot, a real-time search engine, is gaining momentum as an aggregator of real-time search from sites like Twitter, Digg, and StumbleUpon.

Where will search go next? It's hard to tell, but one thing we know is that the search engine algorithms are relying more and more on social proof.

90% is getting the headline right

The title of your article, email, or blog post is the most important way to affect search optimization. Why? Because search is shifting towards sharing links (similar to bookmarking sites) and almost all links are shared with the title attached. Furthermore, the headline is the first thing a person sees and is often the only information they have to determine whether they will click to read more. A bad headline alone can be a deal breaker when it comes to sharing!

The good news is you don't need to know much about headline copywriting. You can steal strong heading formats from books, magazines, other people's blog posts, and keyword suggestion tools. Here are some tips for writing smart headlines:

- Write your content before you write your headline

- Create a headline that highlights the best point in your content

Buzz Tip: 102 Proven Headlines for Social Media and SEO

Excerpted from Authority Blogger by Chris Garrett

Get What You Want (Health, Wealth, Relationships, Time and Lifestyle)

1. 10 Money/Time Saving Tips for _____

2. The Secret of Getting the Best Price for Your _____

3. How to Find the Best _____ Deals on the Web

Problems and Fears

1. Are _____ a Dying Breed?

2. How to Beat the Fear of _____

3. 10 _____ Scams and How to Avoid Them

How-To Tricks of the Trade

1. When is it Smarter to _____ or _____?

2. Little Known Ways to _____

3. 10 Reasons it's Better to _____

Download all 102 headlines in PDF format:

http://socialmediaworkbook.com/wp-content/ uploads/102-headline-formulas.pdf

http://authorityblogger.com

- Use your main keywords in your headline

- Borrow a headline format from something really popular, like a movie title

- Be imaginative and catchy, but don't get too clever

- Write something that will encourage people to click (remember, you want a date, not a marriage!)

Additional internet copywriting style tips

Here are a few more reminders about writing internet copy. Many of these you should already know, but this list also serves as a checklist to go through before you create content.

- Choose topics you know about, so you don't frustrate readers with your ignorance.

- Connect topics back to your business, product, or service.

- Make it interesting--nobody wants to get bored when they are reading an online article.

- Keep your content shorter--People online have short attention spans, so give just enough information to make your points quickly.

- Create your own style and add personality and opinion to your work. It's much harder to be someone else than to just be yourself.

- Use the slang of your target audience, it will help you connect with your readers.

- Edit out clichés and topics that have been written

Buzz Tip: List of useful phrases in internet copywriting

- Guaranteed

- Fast

- Limited

- Easy/Simple

- Testimonial

- Free

- Discount

- Sale

- New

- Important

- Partnership forming words like "invest in our product" (instead of "buy" or "purchase")

- Major benefits like "lose weight"

- Direct instructions like "Click here"

about several times already.

• Edit and trim your work, but don't compromise on quality.

• Anticipate objections before you publish, and consider whether you should address the topic within your original content.

• Do not use any outrageous claims in your add copy-- online readers are both savvy and skeptical.

Summary

For every piece of content you write, go back through and optimize with SEO and copywriting best practices.

This includes:

- On-page SEO

- Off-page SEO

- Keyword research

- Headline copywriting

Learn More

Copyblogger (http://copyblogger.com) – Brian Clark has been writing direct-marketing response since the 1990's. He's built three successful online businesses since starting this copywriting blog in 2006.

SEOBook (http://seobook.com) – Aaron Wall and his team wrote the book on SEO. You can learn the latest and most advanced SEO techniques from this blog and subscription website.

SEOMoz (http://seomoz.org) – SEOMoz is another organization that provides free and paid SEO training via its site. I highly recommend subscribing to the blog if you are just getting your feet wet in search optimization.

PR and Advertising

One of the best publicity stunts in the history of launching a company started when Half.com wanted to put their name on the map. They convinced the town of Halfway, Oregon, to rename itself to Half.com, literally putting them on the map!

It took the company six weeks and a budget of $100,000 to make the name change happen, and the change went into effect just hours before the company launched. The publicity that amounted from this stunt was enormous, and the company sold to EBay for $300 million 6 months later.

The internet is an attention-driven marketplace, which means companies must try harder than ever to get noticed. To get attention, consider these guidelines:

- Do something that (literally) no one has ever done before

- Make sure there is some link between your publicity stunt and your product

- Come up with a catchy phrase to make the link to your product obvious

- Be honest and straightforward about your stunt to build trust and gain participation

- Don't bribe others to participate, because it's more authentic when people participate for no reason other than that they want to!

It's not easy to create the kind of buzz Half.com did. However, success breeds more success, so as you plan your successful campaign on social media, it helps to reinforce it with traditional methods, like PR and advertising. With these three forces working together, you will create a ton of buzz. In this chapter, you will learn how to build momentum in traditional media and how advertising on social media sites can boost your success rates.

Create and use press releases

First, understand that if you are not a PR professional by trade and you can afford to outsource your public relations needs, you should. Although press releases are short pieces of content, that does not mean they are easy to write.

If, however, you want to do PR in-house, this chapter is for you. You can create respectable press releases by using the template here, but allow yourself some time to get used to the format.

Press releases should give new information about your business or product. A few years ago, getting press in traditional media usually guaranteed a flood of new prospects to your website or product. But today, traditional press, even in digital form, does not have the power to drive consumers that it once did.

Buzz Tip: PR release template

FOR IMMEDIATE RELEASE:

Contact:

Contact Person

Company Name

Telephone Number

Fax Number

Email Address

Web site address

Headline

General information, including the date and the city and state of origin for the press release

An introductory paragraph that answers who, what, where, when, why, and how.

Middle paragraphs that add support to what is written in your title and first paragraph.

A closing paragraph that ties up any loose ends. Also provide contact information again, including a name, email address, and link where the person can find more information.

But if traditional media cannot drive traffic the way it once did, why would you create a press release? Plenty of reasons. For one, journalists still use press releases to develop their stories. If they write about your company, you will gain credibility and can use that story to land more press. Press in newspapers and magazines is also the first step to getting televised press.

Furthermore, your press release could be republished on news sites in its original form, which would give a link back to your website. When Dan Schawbel published his book Me 2.0, he sent press releases and was featured on over 125 websites the day of his book release. He took his website from a page rank of zero to a page rank of six within 4 months due to all the inbound links, a feat that usually takes two to three years.

To write a press release, use the template provided. Your press release should be as short as possible, preferably under 300 words. Brevity is important, and as they say, the longer you talk the more likely you are to say something stupid. Everyone will appreciate you getting to the point.

Find a reason to send a press release

According to Mark Hughes, author of *Buzzmarketing*, there are five main categories of stories the press will cover. He writes, "If you can create a story with any of these story angles you're going to capture media attention. Create a story that packs two, three, or four of these angles, and you've got a grand slam!"

The five main categories as he describes them are:

- The David-and-Goliath story

- The unusual or outrageous story

- The controversy story

- The celebrity story

- What's already hot in the media

In the spirit of these five categories, here are some questions to ask yourself to find your angle:

- Are you the underdog to someone (anyone)? If you own a small business, you are probably the underdog to someone.

- Are you the youngest person to do something? The oldest? The fastest or fattest or strongest? The press loves "-ests."

- Is your approach to a problem unusual? Does it defy conventional wisdom? Go to your favorite search engine and search for "How to launch a _____." For example, if your product is a book, search for "How to launch a book." Now, choose five things off the list and do the opposite. Tell the press about why you are a genius for doing it differently than everyone else.

- Can you craft a publicity stunt like Half.com renaming a town "Half.com?"

- How far can you push the envelope? What can you do that's controversial, without ruining your brand? To promote this book, I asked several of my friends to dress up in bee costumes with me for Halloween. Unusual and harmless is always a good combination when it comes to being memorable.

- Who is the most well-known person who uses your product? Are they "celebrity" enough to be newsworthy?

Press Release Directory List

Here is a list of both free and paid press release sites where you can syndicate your press releases. The sites are ranked in order of quality for SEO purposes.

- PRNewsWire.com

- BusinessWire.com

- PRWeb.com

- PRLeap.com

- PRLog.org

- PR.com

- OpenPR.com

- 1888PressRelease.com

- NewswireToday.com

- PR-Inside.com

- 24-7PressRelease.com

- EcommWire.com

- TheOpenPress.com

- PressMethod.com

- Free-Press-Release-Center.info

- I-Newswire.com

- How can you get a celebrity to sample your product? The sampling has to be unpaid. Advertisements and endorsements are not newsworthy.

- How can you link your company or product to a celebrity or public figure? Remember, they don't have to endorse you.

- What's going on in the news? How can you link your product to the news?

If you brainstorm through these questions, you should be able to find something newsworthy for your press release.

The obvious caveat to sending press releases is that you can't send them too often, or you will end up in the proverbial circular file. Even traditional media draws the line at unsolicited spam, so send fewer announcements to stay relevant. There are no real guidelines to how often you can send press releases, but six a year is about right.

Pitch Engine is a new way to pitch using short press releases created specifically for social media.

Go to http://www.pitchengine.com/ to learn more.

The press gets social: develop your press release contact list

It's easy to create one press release and submit it to press release directories. But if you want actually to get your story written by a real person, sending targeted releases is a better idea. Here is a guide to who should receive your press release and how should you tailor it:

- National news sources should always be on your list. Send them the best combination of the five most-written-about stories.

- Are there people involved in your story? (That's a rhetorical question – there should always be a personal element to your story.) Local newspapers and other publications from every person's hometown and current town should be on your list. You can also include any publications from their college alma maters. Tailor the release to emphasize the person and his or her involvement with the project.

- Is your product or service location-based? Put news sources from that area on your list, and focus on why your product was just made for people who live in this area.

- Bloggers should not be on your list. Almost all bloggers despise press releases, and are more likely to write about how horribly rude your press release was than about the content of it. Develop personal relationships and use social media with bloggers if you are interested in having them write about your product or service.

You can find contact information by putting together a target list and going to each source's website to find the editors and reporters on staff.

You can also contact the media directly. Twitter is one of the best ways to get the attention of the media because so few people are using it still. Use the Media On Twitter database (http://www.mediaontwitter.com/) to find journalists that meet your criteria. Start by following the person and getting to know them by reading their Twitter stream. You can reply to their tweets to establish a friendly professional relationship. If the person is receptive, you can progress to a pitch through email. If you remind the person that you have already spoken to them, they will be much more receptive to your pitch.

Plus, the media is looking for you! Peter Shankman started an email list called Help a Reporter Out (HARO) in 2008. You can join the list for free (http://helpareporter.com) and receive three emails every weekday with story queries for books, television shows, magazines, newspapers, and online articles.

Build your opt-in email list

You can also send a more personalized version of your press release directly to consumers. Remember how bloggers hate press releases? Well, if you remove the press release jargon (and formatting) and personalize the main content with a name and salutation, you now have a personal message to send out online.

You can use e-mail marketing to spread the word in addition to press releases. If you have an email list already, this is the perfect message to integrate into a newsletter. If not, here is some guidance on building an email list.

Permission is crucial in email marketing. You can get permission by enabling an opt-in through your email service provider so a subscriber can confirm their interest in your email blasts.

Emails can be shared too

The focus of Social Pollination so far has been on social media websites, but email is also a method of sharing information from peer-to-peer. To enhance the chances of your email getting passed on, you can include a postscript at the bottom of your email telling recipients to share the email with friends.

That alone probably won't get you many forwards; you must also give them a good reason to forward the message. Free reports, valuable coupons, and funny content work just as well in emails as they do on social media. You can also use any form of relevant or timely information, research studies, and interactive content like a quizzes or compatibility questionnaires.

Who should be on your list?

- People who want information from you and have opted-in

- Potential customers who have opted-in

- Previous/current customers or members of your site (no need to opt-in because you have a relationship with these people already)

How to entice people to your email list

Many web publishers use what is called a squeeze page to collect email addresses. This is basically just a page that is setup specifically to talk about the benefits of the email list and why someone should sign-up for it. Usually, people are willing to trade an email address (or other contact information) for valuable content.

To create a squeeze page, make sure you include these items:

- Eye-catching title

- Benefits of signing up

- Cost (if any)

- Call to action

- Sign-up box

- Guarantee of privacy

Other best practices include:

- Use your normal website theme or white as the background

- Use a narrow column for the text (600px wide or less)

- Remove any other links on the page

- Remove all sidebars, top bars, footer information

- Build your email list with other people's email lists

In a previous chapter about finding content, we talked about article banks. Not only can you pull articles from these sites to republish, but you can also submit articles for other people to send to their newsletter subscribers. In the resource box, include a link to an email sign-up for a free report related to your article, and you can get several new subscribers if a large newsletter picks you up.

Tip: Use anchor text within your resource box so that you are generating back links based on your keyword phrases.

You can also partner with other newsletters in your industry and offer to trade articles every once in awhile. As long as you are not direct competitors, this trade benefits everyone and increases both of your lists.

Another way to get your message published is with blog aggregation networks. Sign-up is free and you can post articles in the community. These articles may get syndicated to other places on the web.

There are several other lists you can join and participate in. People who are already on email lists are more likely to subscribe to your email list. Search for groups in your industry from these websites:

- ***Email groups on Yahoo and Google*** – There are thousands of people already on email lists between these two web giants. Look for groups relevant to your industry that are moderated. Moderation is important; groups that are not moderated tend to get hit with spammers. Participate in the email group before sending out any promotions. It's polite to send an introductory email whenever you join the group. Once you've established a repertoire with the group, you can share occasional promotional messages as long as they are extremely relevant.

• *Facebook groups* – Administrators are allowed to email the entire group, so if you can convince your administrator that your message is relevant and useful to everyone, you can get free publicity and entice members back to your own email list.

• *LinkedIn groups* – Anyone in the group can start a thread, and all thread topics are emailed to the group depending on each person's privacy settings.

• *Ning groups* – You can message your entire friends list in one fell swoop. Groups also work the same way Facebook groups work – the administrator has the power.

Sponsorships

Sponsoring a social influencer can be a fantastic way to get the word out about your product. The best way to get a blogger to write about you is to offer free samples of your product in exchange for reviews. You may also pay highly influential bloggers to write about you, though some bloggers are wary of this tactic, because it can damage their credibility. Here are some tips for getting sponsorships:

• *Research your targets* – do your homework and make sure that each blogger you are targeting truly fits your target customer. Also, make sure that they types of people who read the blog are also your target customers.

- ***Let the blogger experience your product*** – you must give away a sample of the product at minimum. You must also be open to a criticism or a bad review. Samples are not bribes to say something positive about your company. Two ways to avoid bad reviews are to build the right target list to begin with, and to provide the product with no strings attached at all, meaning that the blogger doesn't have to write about you unless they really enjoyed your product.

- ***Do the work for them*** – make it easy for the blogger to write about you. It takes time to test a product (especially software) and craft a blog post. Provide a walkthrough, or set up an account for the person. Give the person a simple guide to follow or provide a list of key features they could check out. Also, make it extremely clear in your pitch how this product benefits them, and how it would benefit their audience.

- ***Follow up*** – send a thank you message when the post is up. Ask for any additional feedback beyond what was printed. Keep the person on a list and keep them in the loop with new products, updates, and features.

One final note: the Federal Trade Commission requires that all bloggers disclose their relationship with your company. Be sure that the deal you are creating is ethical and within the guidelines of the FTC. You can learn more at http://www.ftc.gov/opa/2009/10/endortest.shtm.

Reinforce your popularity with social media advertising

Despite what I have said so far about advertising being ineffective, I do not believe advertising is completely useless. According to ComScore, social networking sites account for more than 20 percent of all display ads viewed online, with

MySpace and Facebook combining to deliver more than 80 percent of ads among sites in the social networking category. There is clearly an advantage to advertising on social media sites right now, simply because there is so little competition.

When you want to reinforce your message, advertising can be a good compliment to a social media campaign, especially when you advertise on the same channels you use. The difference between ads from search engine companies like Google AdWords and social media companies is that demographics from search engine companies are inferred by on-page content and what other websites a user visits, and demographics from social media companies are given by user-input data. This could be a good or bad thing, depending on what your goals are.

Social media sites supposedly produce lower click-through rates compared to popular ad networks like Google Adwords. Several companies have seen success though when they created highly targeted campaigns based on self-proclaimed interests and social demographics. Campaigns that appeal to the interactive nature of social networks also tend to do better than general advertising campaigns. These types of campaigns include engaging tasks like watching a video or voting. Lightspeed Venture Partners shares one example on their blog:

> "Rockyou ran for Pentel Pens that asked users to enter 'their smoothest (pickup) line' into a sweepstake. The rich media with video campaign led to real engagement with a 22.5% engagement rate (2x av performance for the category), a 0.6% CTR and 60% of users watching at least half of the video."

Advertising on social media websites is still in its early days, but here are a few tips for advertising on some of the biggest social platforms.

MySpace (https://advertise.myspace.com/)

MySpace allows you to create banner ads that show up all over the site. There is no guarantee that the ads will appear above or below the fold, and there is no way to control what types of pages the ads are put on. You can choose between impressions-based advertising (CPM) and performance-based advertising like click-through rates (CTR) and the cost is comparable to a Google AdWords campaign.

Facebook (http://www.facebook.com/advertising/)

Facebook allows you to choose detailed demographic profiles and displays text ads with images in the right sidebar on all pages of the site. You can pay by impressions or clicks and you can even promote pages from Facebook's own site (like your fan page or group). You can also advertise polls, events, or video through Facebook ads.

While the cost of advertising on Facebook is cheaper that Google Adwords, click-through rates on Facebook are lower.

LinkedIn (http://linkedin.com/directads)

If you are targeting a specific industry for professional services, recruiting, or B2B, you can purchase text ads that are guaranteed to display above the fold in relevant groups and profiles from the target demographic you select. You pay by impressions, not clicks, and depending on your target audience, you can pay $3-$20 for 1,000 impressions. You can also advertise indirectly on LinkedIn through Google Adwords.

Some people have said that LinkedIn works well for job postings, but returns abysmal results for general advertising. For general advertising, Google Adwords appears to work only slightly better than LinkedIn Direct Ads.

SlideShare (http://www.slideshare.net/about/advertise)

SlideShare offers a number of advertisement opportunities that will be useful for business and technology companies. These include display ads, custom brand channels, contest hosting, email newsletter ads, custom sponsorship units, presentation featuring, and lead captures.

You can request a media kit to learn more about each of these offerings and how they can work for your business.

StumbleUpon (http://stumbleupon.com/ads/)

You can submit your link to a category and pay $0.05 for every impression to StumbleUpon users in that category. Each user has the option to say they like it, that it's not for them, or keep stumbling without voting.

If you do not have a strong network on StumbleUpon but you know your content could go viral on the site, you can spend $50-$100 to get your link in front of users who will then decide.

Digg (http://digg.com/advertise)

You can contact Digg for advertising rates on their banner ads through the website. I have also seen blended ads embedded into their front page to look like natural digg results, so those types of ads may be more effective than banner ads.

Remember, advertising online always requires good copy and testing. Test ads in small batches before investing high amounts in one campaign run.

Summary

• Use press releases to reach traditional media whenever you can find a great angle

• Incorporate as many of the five types of stories traditional media likes into one press release

• Build your opt-in email list to supplement your social media campaign and press list

• Advertising on social media sites can reinforce a successful social media campaign

Learn More

Steve Rubel (http://www.steverubel.com/) - Steve Rubel is SVP, Director of Insights for Edelman Digital, a division of Edelman, the world's largest independent PR firm.

PRSarahEvans (http://prsarahevans.com/) - Sarah Evans is a consultant and TV personality who provides commentary on daily news and issues in the PR space.

How to Deal with Bad Publicity

In early 2009, two Domino's Pizza employees created an amateur video of themselves coughing and sneezing on a customer's sandwich during work hours. They posted the video on YouTube, and within a day the video had over 1 million hits.

Ramon de Leon, a Domino's operating partner in Chicago, heard about the incident and immediately used Twitter to share reassurances about the employee training standards of the Chicago stores he owned. He also sent individual messages to people in his Chicago network, asking them to share the information with their followers.

The next day, Domino's released a three minute response video with the CEO of Domino's calling what his employees had done a felony. The video was impromptu and the CEO failed to make eye contact with the camera, which made viewers wonder if he was reading from cue cards. The company released this response video on YouTube, where it received a fraction of the views the original video had received.

People criticized Dominos for not responding promptly to the incident, using strong language, coming across as unprofessional and disingenuous, and using the wrong communication channel for the content. On the other hand, people were supportive of Ramon de Leon's approach to handling of the situation in Chicago.

Part of social pollination is accepting that once you release your message on social networks, you lose control over what happens. Someone may not like your company, product, or service and could comment on your social media profiles, or complain about it on a different social media site. Don't let complaints stop your company from using social media, because the conversation is happening whether you are present or not.

Reputation management monitoring

As you plan your social media strategy, include reputation management monitoring. The best way to monitor your company's reputation on the internet for free is by signing up for Google Alerts and using keywords related to your company, like your company's name, competitor's names, and the names of your company's executive team.

Google Alerts is a service that sends you daily emails whenever anyone mentions your name on the internet. It indexes anything and everything that is public, including online news publications, websites, blogs, Twitter, Digg, Facebook, and most other social media sites. Google will catch 99-100% of online mentions of your company.

Brands in Public

by Seth Godin, author of Tribes

I was talking with a senior marketer at one of the most famous brands in the world last week. She said, "executives keep coming to me with stuff they find on the internet, stuff they find on YouTube about us, and say, 'take it down!' Of course, I have to explain that I can't take it down. No one can."

If your brand has any traction at all, people are talking about you. Of course, they've always talked about you, but now they're doing it in writing, in video and in public.

You can't control what people are saying about you. What you can do is organize that speech. You can organize it by highlighting the good stuff and rationally responding to the not-so-good stuff. You can organize it by embracing the people who love your brand and challenging them to speak up and share the good word. And you can respond to it in a thoughtful way, leaving a trail that stands up over time.

Lately, we've seen big brands (like Amazon and Maytag) get caught in a twitterstorm. An idea (one that's negative to the brand) starts and spreads, and absent a response, it just spirals. Of course, Amazon can't respond on their home page (they're busy running a store) and they don't have an active corporate blog that I could find, so where? How?

Enter Brands In Public.

Squidoo offers pages for large brands. Each page collects tweets, blog posts, news stories, images, videos and comments about a brand. All of these feeds are algorithmic... the good and the bad show up, all collated and easy to find.

Of course, these comments and conversations are already going on, all over the web. What we've done is bring them together in one place. And then we've made it easy for the brand to chime in.

If your brand wants to be in charge of developing this page, it will cost you $400 a month. And once you take the page over, the left hand column belongs to you. You can post responses, highlight blog posts, run contests or quizzes. You can publicly have your say right next to the constant stream of information about your brand (information that's currently all over the web-- and information you can't "take down" or censor). You can respond, lead and organize. If a crisis hits, your page will be there, ready for you to speak up. If your fans are delighted, your page makes it easy for them to chime in and speak up on sites around the web.

If you have the tools and wherewithal to build a page like this on your own site, you should consider that. The challenge is getting it done, regardless of where the page lives.

There are already monitoring tools online (like Radian6) that allow big brands to watch from behind the scenes. That's great, but what are you doing in front of your audience? Is there a low-cost, easy way to let one of your non-technical marketing people lead and engage with people who are already in the conversation?

Allstate and Molson and Home Depot see the value of showing up where the conversation is happening. Brands will discover that they can't just rely on a static home page, nor is it sufficient to post an ephemeral response in a feed somewhere. Brands in Public isn't the first, nor will it be the last place brands need to be to coordinate and organize the conversation. People (your customers) will find these pages, point to them, link to them and talk about them, creating a new circle of interest online.

It's worth saying that we care a lot about keeping this simple for your organization. A Brands in Public page for your brand requires no development team, no ad buys and no deep pockets. While you control the left-hand column and can pepper it with good stuff, it's still part of a larger site, not "your" page. That means that the number of meetings you need to go to for approvals and permissions is going to decrease. It means that it's not behind your firewall and not something that has to fit into the larger über-corporate strategy. More like a tradeshow and less like your home page. It's in public. It's simply a place for your brand to see and be seen, to organize and to respond.

I'm guessing that big brands are going to need to be in dozens of places like this going forward, because media has shifted from top down, "here's what we say, we're putting on a show, watch us!" to, "oh, you're here, you're talking, hi."

http://www.brandsinpublic.com/
http://sethgodin.typepad.com/

You can also monitor your brand periodically with OneRiot, which is a real-time search engine that gives up-to-the-minute results from everywhere on the web.

Responding to complaints on social media

If you don't employ a PR agency, you will have to decide how to respond to these complaints within your company. You can handle bad social media publicity in a variety of ways:

- If the complaint is false, calmly and publicly dispel it as soon as you see it.

- If the complaint is valid, work with the person to fix it and share the solution on social media. This puts a positive spin on the incident.

- If the complaint is just a casual remark, ignore it or if it is warranted, email the person privately. Remember that no company or product is the right one for all people. Give your customers' complaints more weight than a casual observer's, and don't obsess over people who are just sharing their opinions on social media.

Queen bees don't fight their own battles

As a company, there's nothing more frustrating than receiving hostile or negative feedback on your products. You want to correct the issue, but none of the steps you are taking seems to neutralize the situation.

Instead of giving up, mobilize your army of loyal customers. Do you know how worker bees protect their queen? Whenever an enemy enters the hive, the worker bees surround the enemy in a tight circle, until the enemy suffocates.

There is no stinging or fighting – just a unified wall that the enemy cannot break through.

Loyal customers are the perfect unified wall against enemies. If your competitor or a disgruntled customer is attacking you unfairly in public, alert your loyal customers to the problem and let them defend you with the truth.

A few more guidelines on responding to complaints using social media:

- Respond as soon as you see the complaint, to help control the message. Remember that word spreads quickly on social media and that viral marketing works for any type of message, not just the positive ones about your company. You can prevent viral complaints by developing relationships with your customers before an incident occurs.

- Respond on the right medium and use the right person from your company to respond. Don't use social media to respond to shareholders or mainstream media. When responding on social media, your CEO may not always be the appropriate choice. Choose the respondent that matches the severity of the complaint, just as you would offline.

- Allow the customer to have their say, but if the customer has a scathing complaint, attempt to handle the problem with email or the phone, instead of social media. The more the person complains on public forums, the harder it is to control the message.

- Show interest by asking the person to explain and respond without getting offensive. Apologize for the inconvenience, even if you don't admit your company was wrong. Get to the heart of the problem and repeat it back to make sure you understand.

- Your response must be genuine and warm. The response should seem casual but not unprofessional, and should be kept short and to the point.

• Be clear about the resolution options, and offer the customer a choice of how he wants the complaint resolved. Summarize the solution you both agree on and publicize it using the original source of the complaint.

• Remember that customer satisfaction depends more on customer experience than having a perfect product or perfect company. If you can make the customer feel good about doing business with you, that matters more than the problem.

Prevention

Use social media to build relationships with your customers as soon as possible. When you make your customers comfortable doing business with you, they are less likely to complain on a public forum. Instead, they will email you and try to work it out offline, and they will remain loyal after the problem is resolved.

Be as optimistic and helpful as possible on social media to set the tone for when your customer has a problem. Build a relationship based on trust. Be approachable and friendly, and you can avoid your customer complaining publicly because she will have no problem contacting you directly, in private.

Listen to your customers when they are not complaining. Get to know who they are, what they like and dislike, and what they need in their daily lives. Use social media to be proactive in finding problems you can solve for your customers.

Use CRM software to check in with customers you have had complaints with in the past. Ask them how you are doing periodically, and whether they have any feedback. When you ask your customers for feedback, you can turn a negative

experience into a positive one and create fiercely loyal customers that are invested in your product or company.

Summary

• Use reputation management tools to monitor what people are saying about your company online

• Respond to complaints on social media using the guidelines set forth in this chapter

• Use social media to your advantage to build relationships with your customers and reduce total complaints

Social Media Tracking and ROI

Think local businesses have no use for social media? Think again. Naked Pizza is an independent healthy pizza joint in New Orleans that serves just a 20 mile radius. In just under three months, the company built a 4,300 person following on Twitter.

Naked Pizza found that as long as its CEO Jeff Leach tweeted between 1 and 15 times every day, 20% of the company's daily sales came from users who entered the site from Twitter. Furthermore, during one particular advertising blitz on Twitter, 69% of the company's sales entered the website from Twitter.

Because Naked Pizza was able to link their use of social media analytics to actual daily sales, the company determined precisely how much return it was getting from its social media use. As a result, Naked Pizza changed its billboard from a phone number to a Twitter handle. Naked Pizza received a ton of press when they changed the billboard, and is now getting funding from Kraft to become a national chain.

So what made Naked Pizza successful? Naked Pizza understood its goals, and found metrics to track its success against those goals. The company set up tracking tools, collected data, and analyzed the results to make a business decision that set them apart from their competition.

There is no point in creating a social media strategy if you are not going to measure the results. According to an August 2009 survey by Mzinga and Babson Executive Education, 86% of professionals have adopted social media, but only 16% currently track return on investment for the programs they run. 40% claim they do not know if they even could track ROI, which implies that social media ROI is not well understood by many professionals.

If you keep your goals from Chapter 2 at the forefront, you can calculate your company's ROI with social media. Metrics are driven by goals. You cannot manage what you cannot measure, so focus on your goals and refine them to make them measurable so you can track your success.

Some of your goals will be easy to measure. When you measure customer support, you want to look at how many issues you resolved over a certain period of time, and how satisfied the customer was with your resolution. The success of your sales pipeline can be measured by how many leads you generate and how many of those leads become one-time or loyal customers. Recruiting can be measured by how many people applied to your job through social media sources vs. traditional sources, and how the quality of candidates differed between the two.

When you get into thought leadership, brand awareness, and brand loyalty goals, things get tricky. You do not want to measure just numbers, but also engagement levels. For these goals, much of the data will be qualitative, making it more difficult to sort and understand.

Measuring qualitative data

There are three categories you want to measure qualitatively on social media: engagement, sentiment, and influence. Although these are soft measurement areas, you can still create and track key performance indicators (KPIs) based on your company's goals.

5 C's of engagement

PostRank measures social media engagement by the 5 C's of engagement:

- **Creating** – Writing content about a brand, primarily with a blog post

- **Critiquing** – Commenting or sharing an opinion about a brand on any social media site

- **Chatting** – Sharing content about a brand with your network

- **Collecting** – Submitting, bookmarking, or voting for content

- **Clicking** – Clicking on a link about a brand that was shared on social media

All 5 C's show that a consumer is engaged, but not all types of engagement are created equal. Postrank reasons that creating content takes more time than critiquing, critiquing takes more time than chatting, and so on down the list.

PR Firms Add No Value?

by Gini Dietrich, CEO of Arment Dietrich

The Business Insider states:

> "I've worked as a senior corporate communications exec for three Fortune 500 companies and I'm confident in saying that 90 percent of PR firms add no value."

When I worked at Fleishman-Hillard in Kansas City, I was on the Ocean Spray account. I loved working on that business. It was a large account and we were doing communication for cranberry juice, which was an easy sell because of the health benefits. We created a campaign calling "The Art of the Ocean Spray Harvest" and commissioned three photographers to depict the cranberry harvest in British Columbia, Wisconsin, and Massachusetts (if you ever visit my office, you'll see three of the commissioned photos framed on my walls).

It was a great campaign. Not only did we create a traveling art gallery, but we were able to sell photos (framed and unframed), postcards, stationery, and other trinkets with the cranberry harvest depicted and donated the proceeds to America's Second Harvest. We gave away tons of samples of juice that year. We worked with city officials. We worked with art galleries in many major cities. And we worked hand-in-hand with the charity.

At the end of the program, we very proudly presented our results to the client. Three six inch binders full of stories that had run, gallons and gallons of juice given away, thousands of dollars donated to the charity... and then it happened.

The client looked at everything very patiently and then shrugged her shoulders and said, "This is great. But our sales are down and this very expensive PR program did nothing for us. We can't afford to keep you guys on next year."

WHAT?! All that work. Fourteen weeks of travel. THREE six inch binders full of stories. And we're being fired?

That was the beginning of the end of my time at FH and the beginning of the time that I began to think there has to be a better way. Now when I hear, "We can't guarantee results" or "We can't make the media write your story" it makes my skin crawl.

The truth of the matter is, especially in today's digital age, the right communication CAN affect the growth of your business. So if you hire us and we tell you news releases don't work, it's because we're not publicists. Your company or your CEO getting an ego stroke because we got you three six-inch binders full of stories isn't going to affect business growth. It's also because we're not going to distribute a bunch of news releases, let the wires pick them up, and then tell you we did our jobs. It doesn't work. Period.

I love it when people change careers and go into PR because "it seems so easy." I say have at it because you're going in that 90 percent that add no value, leaving room for the 10 percent of us who run businesses AND do communication so we know how, and how not, to affect sales.

http://armentdietrich.com

For every interaction you have with consumers, keep in mind their level of engagement. Create different types of content to allow different people to interact. Many people will never share an opinion about your brand in comment form, but they may passively read your company blog posts.

When using social media, remember to monitor your own engagement with your customers. This list is not just a good way to evaluate your consumers, but also a good way to evaluate your engagement on social media platforms. The more engaged you are on social media, the better the results you will get.

Get the tools

PostRank (http://postrank.com) – Free service that ranks online content based on an engagement score.

Facebook Fan Page Insights (http://facebook.com) – Free service that shows metrics on engagement for Facebook fan pages.

TweetStats (http://tweetstats.com) – Free tool where you can break your Twitter usage down by month and set targets for replying and retweeting. This tool gives you a good idea of how you're tweeting so you can set ROI goals based on strategy.

Conversation sentiment

Conversations about your brand mean less if everything said is neutral or negative. You want positive brand mentions, not just widespread brand mentions. Sentiment measures the tone of the conversation and helps answer the question of whether the conversation surrounding your brand is getting friendlier or more hostile over time.

Are three categories of sentiment (positive, neutral, negative) not enough for your company? Katie Paine, CEO of KDPaine & Partners and PR research and measurement expert, classifies content into 27 categories.

According to Paine's system, your company should decide which of these categories helps you reach your goals, and which would detract from your goals. You can score yourself over time by assigning 2, 1, 0, -1, or -2 to each brand mention for your company.

Paine's 27 categories are:

- Acknowledging receipt of information

- Advertising something

- Answering a question

- Asking a question

- Augmenting a previous post

- Calling for action

- Disclosing personal information

- Distributing media

- Expressing agreement

- Expressing criticism

- Expressing support

- Expressing surprise

- Giving a heads-up

- Responding to criticism

- Giving a shout-out

- Making a joke

- Making a suggestion

- Making an observation

- Offering a greeting

- Offering an opinion

- Putting out a wanted ad

- Rallying support

- Recruiting people

- Showing dismay

- Soliciting comments

- Soliciting help

- Starting a poll

Get the tools

Trendrr (http://trendrr.com) – Free tool, then the service cost is $49+ per month. Allows you to track the trends over time, and compare them to other trends over time.

TweetEffect (http://tweeteffect.com) – Free tool that shows you which tweets caused people to add or leave you within 5 minutes of tweeting.

Influence

Influence is a measurement of how far your content travels beyond your immediate network. It is a much better measure of your network worth on social media sites than friend or follower counts, because it shows the loyalty of your network, and to some extent, their engagement with your content.

Influence measures more than just engagement though--it measures credibility and thought leadership among peers and customers. Influence is also a helpful factor in the success of any viral marketing campaign.

Get the tools

Viralogy (http://viralogy.com) – Free tool that ranks people based on influence on their social media accounts.

Feedburner (http://feedburner.com) – Free tool that provides metrics on your RSS feed. The service measures blog reach and counts subscriber hits per day.

Twitalyzer (http://twitalyzer.com) – Free tool that calculates influence for Twitter handles, based on signal, generosity, velocity, and clout.

TweetReach (http://tweetreach.com) – Free tool that tracks how far your tweet went on Twitter when you search with a phrase.

Twinfluence (http://twinfluence.com) – Free tool that measures influence on Twitter.

More qualitative tools

There are several brand monitoring tools your company can use to collect data on engagement, sentiment, and influence across social networks. Each of these tools also offers many other reports, such as authority, demographics, or conversation themes, which is why it's important to understand your company's goals before committing to a service. Here are some tools to consider if you are looking for a total package:

SocialMention (http://socialmention.com) – Free tool.

Techrigy (http://techrigy.com) – Free basic account, then starts at $600 a month.

Scout Labs (http://scoutlabs.com) – Starts at $99 a month.

Radian6 (http://radian6.com) – Starts at $600 a month.

Sentiment Metrics (http://www.sentimentmetrics. com/) – Paid service.

Measuring quantitative data

This is easier to do with sales and customer services usages, while more difficult to do with public relations, marketing, and research and development usages. Here are some metrics to keep in mind when trying to calculate the ROI of various social media sites:

Email

- Landing page conversion percentage

- Number of opens for each email

- Number of clicks of links in each email

- Number of email subscribers who purchase something

Websites/Blogs

- Total number of posts, or average page views per post

- Unique visitors to your site

- Duration of visitor stay

- Returning visitors

- Clicking path for each visitor until he or she leaves your site

- Subscriber and reach counts via an RSS service like Feedburner

- Comment counts per post (measures engagement)

- Downloads of documents (measures engagement)

- Demographics information via a service like Quantcast

Social networking sites

- Number of members in your group or on your company page

- Percentage of items shared on the medium

- Percentage of traffic driven to website from social network

- Built-in analytics on the site

Miniblogging and microblogging sites

- Number of followers or friends

- Number of items shared and re-shared

- Number of people who respond to questions, polls, and so forth

- Percentage of traffic driven to website from social network

- Hitting the main page or not

Bookmarking sites

- Number of votes or tags

- Number of reviews for submitted item

- Percentage of traffic driven to website from social network

- Hitting the main page or not

- Conversion to taking an action after following a bookmark to your website (for example, subscribing to your blog feed)

General tracking tricks

- Use parameters to create a unique URL (http://example.com?source=google)

- Use coupon or promotional codes to track campaigns

- Use passwords to access special content

Website analytics tools

Google Analytics (http://google.com/analytics) – Free, widely-used tool that lets you create over 80 different views of your website data. You can also create customized reports. As part of Google's terms of use, you agree to give them access to your data, which may be a problem for some companies.

Piwik (http://piwik.com) – Free, open source software that collects analytics data similar to Google Analytics. You install the software on the site and host a database for storage. Because the software is open source, you can hire a developer to create your own analytics software. This option may be better for companies that are not comfortable exposing their data to Google.

Mint (http://haveamint.com) - One-time $30 payment for this software download. Mint gives you more immediate statistics than Google Analytics, so you can see faster which links are doing well.

Mixpanel (http://mixpanel.com) - Free trial, then starts at $25 per month. Mixpanel provides funnel analytics, event tracking, and API support, among other things.

GetClicky (http://getclicky.com) – Free account, then starts at $30 per year. GetClicky provides real-time analytics for your blog and Twitter accounts. The focus is on trends over time, and you can only view your data from a year back.

General dashboard of site statistics: http://xinureturns.com/

Social media analytics tools

Objective Marketer (http://objectivemarketer.com) – Paid tool that helps companies run and measure your campaigns, across multiple social media channels including Twitter, Facebook, LinkedIn and YouTube.

Omniture SiteCatalyst (http://www.omniture.com/en/products/online_analytics/sitecatalyst) – Paid tool that helps you measure Web 2.0 effectiveness, improve conversions, and optimize video performance.

TubeMogul (http://www.tubemogul.com/) – Free tool that provides rich analytics and qualitative measures for online video.

Su.pr (http://su.pr) – Free tool from social bookmarking site Stumbleupon that tracks click-throughs and shows how many additional stumbles happen through sharing via a su.pr link. You can post links anywhere, but there is scheduling for Facebook and Twitter accounts. When you use the link shortener over time with enough variance, it will give you suggested posting times for each day of the week.

HootSuite (http://hootsuite.com) – Free tool that allows you track clicks over time through the URL shortener. You can also do brand monitoring on various social networks with this tool.

Competitor research tools

Part of measurement is setting metrics based on your own goals, while part of it is finding out how you stack up to the competition. You gain good insights about your competitors' social media strategy (if they have one) just by keeping track of them online. You can also see what types of metrics they use to measure their success, and incorporate those into your measurement ROI tracking. I highly recommend making competitor research a part of your social media strategy.

Compete (http://compete.com) – Free features, then membership starts at $400 per month. Check out the competitor's visitors, traffic, inbound and outbound keywords and make comparisons between several sites. Use Compete to find the most searched for keywords for competitor's posts and beat the competition in search engines for those keywords.

Quantcast (http://quantcast.com) – Free features, then starts at $ per month. Use the JavaScript tags they provide on your site to get free information about your company's demographics and other sites your target audience might be visiting. You can also research your competitor's demographics and target sites, and find websites whose demographics look similar to yours.

Trendpedia – (http://www.trendpedia.com/) – Free tool that helps you track and compare conversations across the web about you and your competitors.

Google Insights (http://www.google.com/insights/ search/) – Free tool that allows you to see how your brand stacks up to competitors in various regions.

TweetStats (http://tweetstats.com) – Free tool that allows you to understand how your competitors are using Twitter.

Twitt(url)y (http://tritturly.com) – Free tool where you can type in anyone's Twitter handle and get what links they've tweeted. You can click on each link and see the entire conversation for the link.

Summary

You can measure both qualitative and quantitative data on social media using a variety of tools.

Qualitative measurement consists of measuring

- engagement

- sentiment

- influence

Quantitative measurement uses a variety of metrics to evaluate your harder, more easily measured goals.

With both types of data, you should measure your company's key performance indicators with:

- web analytics

- social media analytics

- competitor analysis tools

Learn More

Katie Payne - PR Measurement (http://www.kdpaine. blogs.com/) - Katie writes about news, trends, and techniques track ROI for public relations campaigns.

F.A.D.S. (http://www.spinsucks.com/) - Gini Dietrich and the Arment Dietrich team write about public relations news, trends, and measurement.

More Thoughts on Social Media Measurement

It's difficult to design a specific program to measure ROI through a book, but there are a few other ideas you should keep in mind when planning social media measurement.

The usefulness of research studies

Did you know that the best time to tweet is either 8am, 11am-12pm, 4:01pm, Sunday evenings, or Friday after work? Confused yet? There are several research studies that attempt to figure out when the best times of day to tweet are, but each has identified a different time!

Research studies are fun to read because you can gain a better understanding of social media at the macro-level. The insights found in research studies are also useful for understanding and brainstorming what factors your company might want to consider for its own experiments.

However, broad studies of social media usage are not going to help you that much. What matters is what works for your company, and the only way you can find that is through measurement.

So if you want to know when you should tweet or update your Facebook fan page, set up Google Analytics and start sending out links to your website at varying times throughout the day (To do this experiment well, you need variability, so tweet at all hours, even the early AM). Then, go to custom reports, and set up your report like this:

Metrics: Bounces, Entrances, Exits, Visits, New Visits, Pageviews, Time on Page

Dimensions: Source, Hour of Day (in that order)

When you create your custom report, you can choose any source and see the hours of the day that your links were most successful.

TweetOClock (http://tweetoclock.com/) – Free, just for fun tool to find out when the best time to tweet yourself is. You can also check someone else's handle if you are targeting someone specific.

Seasonality

Not understanding the seasonality of products is another mistake many companies make with measurement. When you see an increase or decrease in one of your goals, do you really understand why it happened? Be sure to adjust for seasonality.

Seasonality is the natural shifts in online activity over time.

For example, around July, there is a boost in traffic for the keyword "fireworks." What most businesses don't realize is that there are similar things with your company and in your industry that are driven by seasonality.

You can take seasonality into account in your measurement by using smart comparisons. If you see a dip in traffic, compare your results with your competitors' traffic. Translate everything into percentages to see if you are above or below the industry average.

Tying your data back to dollar signs

None of your metrics matter if you can't convert them into a dollar measurement. You are investing time and resources, all of which can be converted into dollar amounts. Every good business person knows that if the investment is in dollars, the return must be in dollars too – and the return on investment must be positive to continue the campaign.

Despite the qualitative nature of some data on social media networks, there should be a way for your company to put a dollar amount on your KPIs. According to an EngagementDB 2009 report of the top 100 global brands, brands that are doing well on social media are also doing well financially.

> "While no one yet has the data to determine direct cause and effect, what we do find is a financial correlation between those who are deeply engaged and those who outperform their peers. . . . To be specific, companies that are both deeply and widely engaged in social media surpass their peers in terms of both revenue and profit performance by a significant difference." Source: Engagement DB, Ranking the Top 100 Global Brands

But without clear cause and effect, can you put a dollar

amount on a relationship? Well, why can't you? Ask yourself these questions, as they pertain to your business:

- How many impressions do potential customers need before they make a purchase?

- How do you define the value of a customer?

- What is the ROI on a long-time customer?

- How many more sales do I make with social media links?

- How do you quantify the value of a social media friend or fan?

- Does connecting via social media sites make a fan more likely to buy?

- When someone shares your content, how many **more** followers or clicks do you get?

- How much does it cost to keep a customer happy?

- How much does it cost to make an unhappy customer into a happy one?

Be ruthless about measurement and getting a return on your investment. You owe it to yourself and your company. You may not know the answers to these questions, but you can design your social media program so you can use data to figure them out.

There will always be qualitative data that cannot be easily measured. Try keeping a record of what your company tried on what channels and at what times, then take note of what worked and what didn't so you can modify your social media strategy.

The social network ROI calculator (http://www. frogloop.com/social-network-calculator) - Designed specifically for running fundraising campaigns, but can help companies determine the value of their social networks.

Setting up experiments

This section is a good resource for companies that are already using tools to measure their impact online, and are ready to take the next steps for improvement.

Split testing

A/B testing, or split testing, is where you have a control group and a variable group to see which group performs better among your target audience.

Split testing is one of the best ways to improve your conversion rates, especially if your goal is creating a sales pipeline. Experiments with split testing work best on websites and via email. Because social media is public in nature, it is harder to design a split test for your social media accounts.

Google Website Optimizer (http://www.google.com/websiteoptimizer) – Free tool that helps you choose pages to split test, test each design alternative with customers, and learn which changes are driving the most conversions.

AWeber (http://aweber.com) - Email service that starts at $20 per month. AWeber lets you split test email sign-up forms and also allows you to split test emails and segment your newsletter subscribers.

User interface testing

As marketing and technology converge into the digital space, a website's user interface plays a major role in attracting and

Case Study: How Daily Burn improved their homepage conversion rate (visitor to sign-up flow) more than 20%

by Tim Ferriss, author of
The 4-Hour Workweek

Along with Founders Fund (Dave McClure), Garrett Camp (CEO, StumbleUpon), and others, I am an investor in Daily Burn, one of the premier diet and exercise tracking sites.

The first step was simple: remove paradox of choice issues.

Offering two options instead of six, for example, can increase sales 300% or more, as seen in the print advertising example of Joe Sugarman from The 4-Hour Workweek. Joe was, at one time, the highest-paid copywriter in the world, and one of his tenets was: fewer options for the consumer.

DailyBurn (DB) was two founders at that point in our conversation, so instead of suggesting time-consuming redesigns, I proposed a few cuts of HTML, temporarily eliminating as much as possible that distracted from the most valuable click: the sign-up button.

Test 1 Conversion Rates: Original (24.4%), Simplified

(29.6%), Observed Improvement (21.1%)

Test 2 Conversion Rates: Original (18.9%), Simplified (22.7%), Observed Improvement (19.8%)

Conclusion: Simplified design improved conversion by an average of 20.45%.

To further optimize the homepage, I then introduced them to Trevor Claiborne on the Google Website Optimizer (GWO) team, as I felt DB would make a compelling before-and-after example for the product. Trevor then introduced DB and me to David Booth at one of GWO's top integration and testing firms, WebShare Design.

The landing page identified for this test was identified as: http://www.gyminee.com

This A/B/C test included three distinct page versions, including the original (control) homepage as well as two variations designed with conversion marketing best practices in mind.

****

Using Google Website Optimizer, the team was able to improve the conversion rate another 16%. To see the full test and results, visit:

http://www.fourhourworkweek.com/
blog/2009/08/ s12/google-website-optimizer-
case-study/

keeping consumers. You can do split testing on your user interface as well as just analyzing the design of your site. Here are some affordable tools that can help your company do UI testing:

UITest (http://uitest.com) – Free tool that provides several different tests for user interface and design of any URL you enter.

CrazyEgg (http://crazyegg.com) – Tool starts at $9 a month. Use CrazyEgg to see where people's eyes go when looking at your page. This tool is essential for testing site redesigns or copy on various pages.

Understanding behavior at the individual level

In many cases, the roll up of information in analytics packages creates a loss of data. If you want to understand trends in your data, consider interpreting each person's data separately, and then putting consumers into segments and analyzing them that way. Trending is very difficult to do on a macro level, and segmentation is an important aspect of making business decisions.

If you have a background in statistics, consider the possibilities of using linear regression to analyze your data. Linear regression techniques are well beyond the scope of this book, but if you know a statistician, you can use analytics software like Piwik to build your database, and export it to Excel or Minitab to analyze.

You can also use a CRM system to track relationships on an individual level. It's possible that a customer who follows you on several different social media sites is more loyal or spends more money than someone who is only connecting with you on one, or someone who is not connecting with you on social media at all.

BatchBook (http://www.batchblue.com/) – Pricing starts at $10 per month. A CRM that has a section for Twitter usernames, blog feeds, LinkedIn profile URLs, and more on each contact record.

Gist (http://gist.com) - Free CRM that focuses specifically on social media. The main downside is you are not able to export your contacts, which would make it hard to do any advanced analysis.

Batchbook and most other CRM systems uses .csv files to import and export contacts. Here are some tools to help you export your contacts from social media sites to .csv files.

- Facebook - Use the Facebook Fonebook app

- Twitter - Use MyTweeple (http://mytweeple.com)

- LinkedIn - Directly from the site (http://www.linkedin.com/addressBookExport)

Need more help? I'd love to help you out.

Email me: monica@monicaobrien.com and I will answer your questions through email or my blog.

The dangers of data-driven marketing

I am a huge advocate of using data to make business decisions, but some companies I have worked with take it too far.

For example, one software company provides an option to upload a special type of document to a person's profile. The company found a correlation between people who upload

Buzz Tip: How to measure your Twitter network

The overarching question is: what makes a Twitterer in your community valuable? Look at just one of your Twitterers to get an idea. There are certainly many different opinions about what factors could contribute to a Twitterer's value to you, but I've narrowed these down to eight major factors and tools to help analyze your current Twitter stream:

Whether the Twitterer tweets about topics you're interested in

This is the first and foremost reason you would want to follow anyone. If the information a Twitterer tweets is relevant to you, then you are gaining value in the form of information, even if you don't interact with the person. NOTE: If the Twitterer does not tweet about topics you're interested in, they detract value from your community because they add noise with their tweets.

Tools: WeFollow, Mr. Tweet, TwitterPacks, Twellow, LocalTweeps

Bonus Tip: List yourself at each of these sites while there!

Whether the Twitterer follows you back

Without a Twitterer who is following you back, you don't have much of a valuation. I know some people will disagree with me on this one, but my argument is if someone is following you back, there is an opportunity for them to see your messages. If they are not following you back, you may as well not exist to them. Clearly, someone who is following you back is worth more than someone who is not.

Tools: Twitter Karma, Tweepular, Huitter, Qwitter, SocialToo

How often the Twitterer tweets

Engagement is vital to the success of the Twitter community. A Twitterer who tweets often probably pays more attention to their Twitter stream, which means they are more likely to interact with you on Twitter. Heavy users also share more information with you, and are less likely to become a stagnant account that hasn't updated in awhile.

Tools: MyCleenr, TweetLater, UnTweeps

How often the Twitterer tweets @ replies

If a Twitterer has a high percentage of @ replies in his or her tweets, this is also a good indication of how engaged the user is with the Twitter community. A more engaged user should have a higher valuation to you.

Tools: TwitterAnalyzer

Bonus Tip: Good for many other stats on you or your friends too!

How often the Twitterer retweets (RT)

One of the greatest values of having followers is when they retweet the content that you've written. The Twitterers who retweet others' content most often should have a higher valuation to you.

Tools: RetweetRank, Twinfluence, Retweetist, Twitturly, Tweetmeme

How often a Twitterer @'s or RT's YOU

They say past performance is a good indicator of future performance. So it follows that if someone has retweeted or replied to you in the past, they may be more likely to do this in the future.

Tools: TwitterSearch

Whether the Twitterer tweets about the same topics you tweet about

If a Twitterer does retweet, the chance of that Twitterer retweeting you depends on whether the two of you tweet about the same topics. If you do, your chances of getting retweeted by this person will be higher than if you don't share the same topics.

Tools: TwitterSheep

Whether the Twitterer's followers are similar to your followers

If the Twitterer's followers are completely the same as your followers (extremely unlikely) and he retweets you, it's essentially like you tweeting the same thing twice. So you can see how the more alike your set of followers are, the less reach you are getting from one follower retweeting you. At the same time, when a message is endorsed over and over again by multiple sources in the same community, that creates buzz within the community. There could be a positive effect rather than a negative one here.

Tools: TwtrFrnd, WhoFollowsWhom, FriendOrFollow

Find more useful Twitter tools at OneForty (http://oneforty.com/), the ultimate database of unique Twitter applications.

documents and people who pay for the service.

So they made the document upload a paid feature, thinking people would be more likely to upgrade for use of that feature. Does this really make sense though?

First of all, correlation and causation are two very different things. Correlation **does not** imply causation. In fact, statistics generally cannot help you find causation, because there just isn't a formula for that.

Second, isn't it possible that due to providing the upload for free, the company was able to convert the customer to a paid suscriber? The feature could have been the company's big selling point, and now they may be seeing less conversion because users can't trial the product fully.

More data is almost always a good thing. Collect and use data, but don't become a slave to it, and don't rely purely on data to drive insight into human behavior. When you pair data with good business sense and intuition, you have a much better chance of making the right decision.

Summary

- Beware of relying on high level research studies to understand your consumers – rely on your own analytics instead

- Keep seasonality effects in mind when measuring successes and failures

- Always tie your data back to dollar signs

- Design your experiments with split testing and user interface testing

- Look at customers individually, then group them into segments for analysis

- Don't rely **just** on the data - pair data with other disciplines when making business decisions

Building a Team

You have a lot to think about when it comes to planning a social media strategy and a viral marketing campaign. A company that is serious about social media will probably want a digital marketing professional or team of specialists to handle its campaigns at some point. There are three ways to handle your social media workflow: hire someone, outsource the work, or automate your processes.

Hiring

Should you hire a consultant, or should you do your social media in-house?

Business Week recently published a survey of 114 members of The CMO Club. The survey found that when considering who should run a social media effort:

- 65.6% preferred in house

- 15.6% preferred a interactive agency

- 9.4% preferred a PR firm

- 9.4% preferred a social media agency

- 0% preferred a creative/ad agency

Furthermore, according to Gartner, 45% of companies have assigned at least one person to manage social media full-time, which implies that dedicated social media positions are on the rise.

You should only hire a consultant for one of two reasons:

- To oversee social media marketing for your company and help you stay on track with strategy. When you start, you can perform many of the tasks yourself or ask your current employees to help you out. You may want to hire a consultant just to have some guidance from an expert.

- To fix a huge problem you are having with social media. Since you've already read this book, you should have no problems getting started in social media, and you can always ask me for help with any social media problems you are having via email: monica@monicaobrien.com.

Social media is time consuming, but it is not that unusual for small companies to have a person dedicated to cost-effective marketing and PR efforts. When your current employees cannot maintain your social media accounts, you should hire someone on a permanent basis. Consultants should never maintain your social media accounts, and agencies are not necessarily the best option for a small business.

If you do decide you need more help with creating or executing a social media strategy, here are some questions you can ask potential consultants, agencies, or new hires:

- **What can you do for my company?** If the person

gives you a list of ideas and tools right off the bat, you probably do not want to work with him. Instead, he should ask you, "Well, what are your goals?"

- *Can I see examples of your work?* Check out corporate blogs and social media accounts the person has managed. Does the person's past work fit your company's style?

- *What experience do you have?* Social media does not happen in a vacuum. If you are a software company, the person should have corporate experience in software. Remember, this person will need to understand the nuances of your industry before he can help you with your social media strategy.

- *Can you describe a time when you met a client's goal--the situation, tasks and actions you performed, and results?* The person should be able to talk about the specifics of a successful campaign they ran that met a previous client's expectations.

- *How do you go about pitching bloggers?* A good answer is "by building relationships with them first." If the person talks more about sending press releases, he probably will not be effective.

- *What is your philosophy on measurement?* This question helps you understand how this person is going to manage your campaign.

- *How do you monitor brands online?* This person should have experience with monitoring tools beyond Google Alerts.

- *Where can I find you online?* Someone who is great at social media for companies can also produce results on her personal accounts.

- *For consultants and agencies: do you accept*

short-term contracts? Do not get locked into a long-term contract. Take some time to see, first, whether the person can deliver results.

Beyond these questions, one other obvious indicator is whether you like the person. Based on your impressions of the person, can this person build relationships with potential customers? Passion and enthusiasm are essential for social media as well. The person should be passionate about your industry and understand your target consumers.

Putting a team in place

It helps to start your social media work with just one member - a champion of social media who can set up accounts, experiment with content, and develop initial relationships. Eventually the work may become too much for just one person, so here are some guidelines for building a social media team.

Put processes in place first

When your company is ready to expand the team, have your champion map out the processes she executes every day, so the work can be distributed more evenly to the group.

Separate tasks by goal

We've talked about seven goals that social media can satisfy, and various members of the team will be interested in various aspects. Your marketing person may be interested in branding, while your IT person may think customer support is the way to go. When you divide the tasks by goal, you can expand your ability to use social media for a variety of solutions.

Use training to accelerate learning

There are several people and blogs listed throughout this book that can help you develop training programs for your employees. This book is also a good resource for introducing people to social media and providing a framework for social media that will get employees in the right mindset from the get-go.

Create social media guidelines

Most business processes have guidelines and social media is no exception. Use ideas from the following companies to create your social media guidelines:

- IBM (http://www.ibm.com/blogs/zz/en/guidelines. html

- Intel (http://www.intel.com/sites/sitewide/en_US/ social-media.htm)

- 38 More Companies: http://laurelpapworth.com/ enterprise-list-of-40-social-media-staff-guidelines/

There is also an excellent free EBook called Building a Social Media Team from Amber Naslund at Alititude Branding. Her two most important points are:

- Build a cross-functional team, including representatives from customer service, product development, business development (sales), public relations, marketing, human resources, IT services, and legal services.

- Create a social culture in your organization, where many of your employees have social media profiles on behalf of the company. This helps with employee attrition and turnover, so your customers don't leave if your social media champion does.

Read the full ebook at: http://altitudebranding. com/2009/09/the-social-media-team-ebook/

Outsourcing

Outsourcing is useful once you have a system in place. You might have your social media strategy set and only need someone to keep the fire going, especially if you have limited participation in social media. Outsourcing is also good for boring tasks that would be a poor usage of your time to complete. Other benefits include:

- No need for extra office space

- No benefits or vacation expenses

- No payroll taxes

Outsourcing social media is a slippery slope, and one that many people disagree about. It is unlikely that you would outsource your entire social media campaign, because you always need someone who is knowledgeable about your company and industry to direct the social media strategy.

If you choose to outsource, the key to outsourcing is having a good template. You must have the process you use down to a science, and you must be able to articulate rules and guidelines to the person you outsource to.

For a cost-effective solution, you can find college interns in your area by posting an ad on Craigslist or Elance. If you choose to go the virtual route, here are a few options:

Virtual Assistant (http://www.virtualassistant.org/)

– Starts as low as $7 per hour for general administrative tasks.

Amazon Turk (http://mturk.com) – A service for completing human intelligence tasks (HITS). Starts at $0.05 per HIT. You can use this for outsourcing mundane list-compiling or database-building tasks.

Automation

Should you automate portions of your social media accounts? It really depends on the medium. For example, a welcome email from an auto responder service is perfectly acceptable in social media. An automated welcome message on a social networking site like Twitter is not. Both are welcome messages, but one is acceptable and the other is considered spam.

Before considering automation, you must understand how others interact on the tools you are using, and follow suit. Every time you join a new social networking site, tread as if it is a foreign country that may have different customs than you are used to. Be on your best behavior and spend more time listening at the beginning. Ask those in your network for help and ideas about what tools you can use.

Here are a few socially acceptable services you can use to automate parts of your social media accounts:

Email

There are countless email services that allow you to run email campaigns, but here are a few I have worked with:

- AWeber (http://aweber.com)

- Emma (http://myemma.com)

- IContact (http://icontact.com)

Content

Posterous (http://posterous.com/autopost) – Free social media site that lets you post content to several social media accounts with just one email. You can email images, blog posts, chats, and just about anything else to all your social media accounts.

PostLater (http://postlater.com) – Paid service, starts at $20 per month. Schedule posts ahead of time to a variety of social media sites, including Tumblr, Twitter, and Friendfeed.

SocialOomph (http://socialoomph.com) - Free service to schedule tweets ahead of time. Premium upgrade with prices starting at $30 per month. From the makers of PostLater.

Ping.fm (http://ping.fm) - Free service that allows you to update your status on several sites at once.

TubeMogul (http://tubemogul.com/) - Free service that allows you to update your video posts on a variety of sites.

Feeds

Feeds are your friend. Most social media sites let you import any feed to your profile page. This helps automate the task of posting blog posts on every social media account you own.

Yahoo Pipes (http://pipes.yahoo.com/) – Free service that lets you aggregate several feeds into one feed. There are many ways to manipulate the final feed to suit your purposes.

Twitterfeed (http://twitterfeed.com) – Free service that lets you push links from a feed to your Twitter account.

Summary

We talked about three ways to execute your social media strategy:

- Hire
- Outsource
- Automate

Closing Words

If I've done my job well, the end of this book should be the beginning of your company's journey using social media to take your business to new levels.

Feel free to contact me with ANY questions or discussion points you have about social media or the content of this book. Really! I think of this book as just an introductory course on what we can learn together. I am happy to answer questions through email or via my blog. Here are the best ways to contact me, in order of preference:

Email: monica@monicaobrien.com

Blog: http://blog.monicaobrien.com

Twitter: @monicaobrien

Finally, I have one favor to ask of you: if you found value in this book, please share it with others!

Thank you for your support.

About the Author

Monica O'Brien is a marketing consultant specializing in results-driven marketing strategy at the juncture of new media and traditional marketing. She spent years doing marketing and PR for startups and small businesses before launching Juncture Marketing consultancy. Now, she teaches solopreneurs, startups, and small businesses how to establish an online presence using new media.

Monica is a Chicago Business Fellow at the University of Chicago. In 2009, she graduated from the Chicago Booth School of Business MBA program with concentrations in marketing, strategy, and entrepreneurship. Monica also holds a Bachelor's degree in Computer Science, with a minor in Physics, from Truman State University.

Monica lives in Chicago, Illinois with her husband and her Westie dog.

Index

C

D

E